CRYSTAL BALL RECRUITING

THE PREDICTIVE GUIDE TO HIRING TOP SALES PROFESSIONALS

ATTRACT | RECRUIT | RETAIN

JASON HOWES

Cover design: Ultimate World Publishing
Layout and typesetting: Ultimate World Publishing
Editor: John Coomer
Illustrations: Tuba Shahbaz
Cover image copyright: Nichcha-Shutterstock.com

ULTIMATE WORLD PUBLISHING
—— PUBLISHING ——

Ultimate World Publishing
Diamond Creek,
Victoria Australia 3089
www.writeabook.com.au

Testimonials

I'd highly recommend *Crystal Ball Recruiting* to anyone hiring salespeople, it will change the way you recruit. Jason Howes understands our needs because he's built and led sales teams himself. He shares real sales stories and offers innovative ways to avoid hiring the same type of reps. He doesn't rely on industry experience alone, he uses predictive, sales-specific data to find coachable, high-performing candidates who hit the ground running.

The Crystal Ball Process is like having the answers before the exam starts. Every hire feels stronger than the last. "These are senior people who know their craft. They've raised the bar across the board, showing us what 'good' really looks like.

Brendan O'Shea
National Sales Manager – Knotwood ANZ

Having utilised the Sales DNA Assessment tool for several years, I can confidently say it's one of the most effective ways to uncover both strengths and development areas in sales professionals. Its flexibility to align with market strategy and required competencies makes it a standout resource.

The tool's ability to reveal hidden gaps—those critical deficiencies in Sales DNA that often go unnoticed—strongly reflects the insights shared in *Crystal Ball Recruiting*. I highly recommend reading this book to discover how you can transform recruitment decisions and long-term sales performance.

Robert Fuller
GM Sales – Australasia

In most organisations, most leaders are expected to sell, yet few feel confident doing it. Sales is too often labelled pushy or transactional, and often working to unrealistic expectations, when in fact the best outcomes come from authentic connection, empathy and persistence.

Leaders must rethink how they value and measure success in sales: align incentives, remove recruitment bias, and recognise the human side of selling. When salespeople feel respected and supported, for both results and relationships, engagement rises and staff turnover falls. *Crystal Ball Recruiting* gives leaders a practical, data-backed framework to attract, assess and develop authentic sellers who perform and stay.

Naomi Herzog
Principal – Business Development
Thomson Adsett

Over the years, I've refined my hiring approach, prioritising mindset, ownership, and attitude over teachable skills. Jason Howes' book *Crystal Ball Recruiting* reinforces these principles and adds the science behind them. It brings structure to the behavioural side of recruitment, helping validate gut instincts with data-backed testing. That gave me real confidence in shortlisting strong candidates. Jason's process also ensures cultural fit, finding people who align with your values, pace, and way of working. I've made costly hiring mistakes before, but I committed to learning from them. Jason's approach helps you avoid those missteps altogether. It's a smarter, more confident way to recruit.

Craig Armstrong
CEO, Mortim Australia

Crystal Ball Recruiting challenged the industry's conditioned mindset of 'I've got this' when recruiting salespeople, exposing the costly reality of time-poor leaders filling roles with urgency rather than strategy. By applying Jason's method, we attracted the right candidates, aligned them with purpose, and onboarded with clarity—making recruitment efficient, effective, and effortless.

Leo Santini
General Manager
ShapeCUT Steel, Stainless & Aluminium Profile Cutting

I worked with Jason Howes for 14 years across two companies, watching him rise from junior trainee to key account manager. His persistence, foresight, and customer-first mindset consistently delivered results and inspired those around him.

Jason helped shape KPIs that drove profitable growth, improved customer retention, and revealed misaligned roles—benefiting both the business and its people. He's always been the trusted advisor in my sales teams.

Crystal Ball Recruiting is a must-read for CEOs and sales leaders seeking a proven blueprint for hiring high-performing sales professionals.

Peter Dallimore
ex-Director, Coastway Timber,
ex-State Manager, Hyne Timber.

I've seen how a salesperson's success often hinges on what happens before they start. *Crystal Ball Recruiting* nails it — it's not just about hiring talent, it's about setting them up to win. Top performers want clarity: KPIs, territory, structured onboarding and strong leadership.

It validates what many of us know but few companies execute — strong candidates ask tough questions before they sign a contract because they care about results.

Jason Howes shows how to attract, support, and retain the top 20% while exposing a blind spot — many sales managers aren't trained in recruitment. *From flawed hiring to shifting goalposts and inaccessible systems.* The case studies are painfully familiar. If you're serious about building a high-performing team, this book is your blueprint.

Jess Jorgenson
Sales Director, Veriforce

This system flat-out works. I've spent years helping companies find the right people and people find the right companies. This playbook nails it. It helps businesses hire smarter, faster and better, with the kind of fit that lasts. If you want to attract top talent and build truly unstoppable teams, this is it.

Pam Foster
Head of Talent Marketing, Career Stylr

Dedication

To my beautiful daughters, Charlize and Sienna—your light, laughter and love are the heartbeat of everything I do. This book is for you, a reminder that dreams are worth chasing and that courage lives in every step forward.

To my parents, Ian and Gail, thank you for your unwavering support and the values you instilled in me. To my sister Lisa, my biggest fan since day one—your belief in me has been a constant source of strength.

To my mentors, Peter Dallimore and Peter Hyne—what I learned from you both set me on an incredible career path. I loved getting some massive deals across the line together. To Peter Eaton (RIP), my squash coach and fiercest competitor—thank you for sharpening my edge, a mindset that's shaped my sales journey.

To the sales professionals and leaders that I've worked with, recruited and connected with over the past 35 years, thank you for your partnerships and friendships. Sales is a blend of art and science, driven by grit and a commitment to solving real problems. Be in the moment. Look and listen closely.

To those who never stop sharpening their arrow through training, reflection and the relentless pursuit of mastery— may your trajectory always be true and your targets always worth hitting. Remember, when you've earned the right, never hesitate to ask for the order.

Contents

Preface

When I first stepped into the world of sales recruitment, I was driven by one simple question: why do so many companies settle for average salespeople when the top 20% are out there, ready to transform results? That question became my obsession—and eventually, my mission.

Over the years, I've worked with hundreds of leaders, HR managers and business owners who were frustrated by hiring mistakes, underperforming teams and the elusive nature of sales success. I've seen first-hand how the right salesperson can elevate a business—and how the wrong one can cost it dearly.

This book was born from those experiences. It's a culmination of the lessons I've learned, the best tools we use, and the mindset shifts that changed everything. Crystal Ball Recruiting isn't just a guide—it's a call to action for leaders who want to recruit using science and data to build stronger teams, and to finally understand the ROI behind every sales hire.

Inside, you'll find case studies, simple checklists, and practical tools to:

- Cut through noise and identify sales talent with true potenial.
- Avoid costly mis-hires that drain time and money.
- Build a leaner, higher-performing team that drives sustainable growth.

Whether you're a seasoned executive or a founder building your first sales team, my hope is that this book helps you see recruitment not as a gamble, but as a strategic advantage. Because when you recruit with clarity, confidence and a crystal-ball mindset, you don't just hire salespeople—you build a legacy.

If you've ever wished you could see the truth about a candidate before you signed the contract, this book is the next best thing.

I'm grateful to those who helped shape this journey.

Let's get started.

Acknowledgements

Writing *Crystal Ball Recruiting* has been one of the most rewarding and revealing growth-filled experiences of my career. It wouldn't have been possible without the support, encouragement and inspiration of many incredible people.

To my clients, thank you for trusting me with your teams, your challenges and your vision. Your commitment to excellence and your willingness to rethink recruitment have shaped both every insight in this book and our mission to recruit the top 20% of sales professionals. You've helped turn ideas into impact and sales stories worth sharing.

To Brendan O'Shea, Naomi Herzog, Jess Jorgensen, Craig Armstrong, Leo Santini and Pam Foster, and all the sales professionals I interviewed (you know who you are)—thank you for your creative input, honest feedback and ability to challenge me in all the right ways. You made this book sharper and more authentic.

This book wouldn't exist without the thousands of candidates who apply for roles with us each year, and the hundreds we interview in search of that "perfect match". Recruitment isn't just about compatibility—it's about alignment. With 70% of candidates feeling jobs are misrepresented, our work focuses on aligning expectations from every angle to improve longevity. I'm especially grateful for our partnership with Objective Management Group and the tools that help bring our crystal ball to life.

To my daughters, my family and my old school mate, Paul Brent—thank you for your patience while I travelled around Australia and Thailand writing this book over the past 12 months. Your unwavering support gave me the space to write, reflect and grow. You reminded me why this work matters—and why leaders need to benefit from it.

And finally, to every sales leader, HR manager, business owner or CEO who's ever asked, *"How do I find the right salesperson who will make me money?"*—this book is for you.

About the Author

Jason Howes is the founder and Managing Director of Arrow Executive Sales, a recognised authority on building high-performance sales teams. With over 35 years of front-line experience, Jason has closed multimillion-dollar contracts and helped leaders to rethink how they hire, train and retain top sales talent.

In 2018, he left the corporate world to solve two persistent challenges: ineffective sales training and the overreliance on "industry experience" in recruitment. Today through his consulting and training, Jason equips leaders with proven systems that deliver measurable ROI—by developing top performers and recruiting salespeople who can truly sell.

Jason is passionate about helping leaders to secure top-tier sales talent. He believes winning your dream clients requires the right people, systems, processes and strategy. A lifelong student of the game, Jason is always learning and bringing the best tools and techniques to the table.

His debut book, *Crystal Ball Recruiting*, distils decades of insights and sales-specific data into a practical guide for hiring with more science and less guesswork. He also hosts the *Sales Trajectory podcast* where he explores innovation, leadership and the future of sales.

Jason lives in Brisbane with his two daughters.

INTRODUCTION

The Sales Performance Crisis

Right now, we're in a sales talent shortage crisis. The average salesperson's tenure is just 18 months and dropping as seasoned sales professionals look towards retirement or are losing the motivation to drive new business opportunities.[1]

Things are heading in the wrong direction, but let's just not blame the salespeople.

Many sources indicate that roughly 50% of sales hires fail.[2] Some reports show that the failure rate is as high as 75%.[3] And I'd consider the failure rate in startups is even worse especially in early-stage or venture-backed companies.

Each salesperson is a $200,000 investment, so you really want to make sure that you're getting a return on that investment. It will make or break you quickly.

But if you're thinking that just by hiring a salesperson, they're going to turn up and miraculously fix all your problems, then you might want to think again.

Some people say you should hire slow and fire fast.

But if you're hiring slow and other companies are hiring fast, then you've got a good opportunity to lose a good candidate from your job.

I would prefer to hire with confidence backed by the right science and data as quickly as you can, but not to rush. You don't want to be hiring just to get someone on a seat. It's a long-term investment in your business.

But most of us have not been trained to recruit for sales, and even some HR (human resource) people are not specialists in sales recruitment, many would admit that. They tend to lean more on the sales leader or hiring manager who potentially doesn't know much either. You'll find typically when you grow to be a company of 50 people, perhaps you may get a part-time HR person. But they're often more involved in other HR activities like documentation and policies.

It's not uncommon, like myself, to end up, you know, at the ripe old age of 33, managing a national sales team. I was involved in some recruitment but never had to recruit myself. And I think this is one of the biggest issues we have even as business leaders—we're juggling so many balls.

One of our valued clients said this about his first experience with sales management and recruiting.

"I went with the standard, more cost-effective route—thought I'd just recruit some BDMs myself and see how it goes."

"One of them worked out well, but a few didn't—they've since exited the business. It was a real learning curve for me. I realised I've got a gap in my skill set when it comes to identifying the right people in the right way."

—Brendan O'Shea, National Sales Manager, Knotwood Australia and New Zealand

We can get caught up in the moment of trying to hire somebody that somebody knows, who's miraculously looking for a job right now, and then you give him or her a go, based on gut feel.

And how are we expected to recruit effectively when salespeople have become very good at interviewing because they've had plenty of practice, right? Candidates can talk the talk, but very few consistently walk the walk.

Right now, what we need is a disruption of traditional methods of hiring, and that's what we've been doing at Arrow Executive Sales over the last seven years.

We are challenging traditional recruitment practices by leveraging online platforms, AI data driven approaches to find and hire sales talent.

This book is like the Uber of sales recruitment because if you look at the impact that Uber made on traditional taxis when they came to the market, they fixed a lot of problems.

Taxis were slack, they were expensive. They weren't clean. They were old. You didn't know when they'd turn up, it was all guesswork (like hiring a salesperson, or even worse, guesswork hiring a sales manager).

Taxis didn't really care because they dominated the market. But Uber disrupted the industry, and the taxis had nowhere to go. They were defeated, and still are.

When we started doing our recruitment, if I wasn't doing anything different from traditional companies, then I didn't bring anything different to the table.

So, we brought the best technology and innovative approaches to take the guesswork out of sales recruitment.

We've been able to scale and use disrupting recruitment methods to uncover more talent, and to make sure that talent can sell before they start the job. Sometimes, finding a "diamond in the rough".

Using science that's backed over 110,000 hires over the last 35 years, we're hiring quality sales professionals who don't have only industry or related product experience.

If you've read Seth Godin's *Purple Cow* book, it's one of my favourites. Godin explains that to survive in today's world, a company needs to have a purple cow—a remarkable idea, a product, a service that will differentiate them from their competitors. Remarkable ideas stand out and people talk about them.

The value, the technology and data that's available before you hire someone is what *Crystal Ball Recruiting* stands for, because I'm passionate about bringing the best people to the table —sales professionals who are hungry, who will win you new business and who will make you money.

One of the biggest challenges that business leaders have right now is that a lot of hiring managers don't have time to recruit. Too much confidence is being put into sales leaders and hiring managers who have never been taught how to recruit. They can't attract quality candidates because most top-quality sales professionals are not actively looking for a job now.

That's why we help craft an employee value proposition to attract the top 20% to your business. If you're not attracting top talent to start with, how can you pick the best?

We help our clients to attract the best.

Hiring managers typically hire salespeople based on their industry experience or market-leading company experience. But having experience doesn't mean they've got sales ability.

We prefer a person with sales ability, and a strong and positive sales mindset who can learn your product. It's much easier, trust me.

If you put too much bias into your hiring and not enough science, then you will tend to hire the same type of salespeople. And if you hire fast and hire on gut feel and bias, then you've got a big problem coming.

If you sit back in a meeting and look around, you can see if there's a lot of people with a similar attribute. They might be a bit fired up or chilled, maybe barrack for the same football team, or be people you'd have a beer with. But are they getting you the results you need?

If your sales aren't growing and your new business development is non-existent, then potentially you've got too many of the same type of people.

THE SALES PERFORMANCE CRISIS

You must take the responsibility of investing in your sales team, systems and processes, and not simply tolerating underperformance. Key questions to ask include:

- What does our team look like right now?
- What's working?
- What isn't working and needs to change?

Instead of procrastinating or thinking a miracle is going to happen, you need to make the hard calls. That's what we love doing when we work with companies.

You're reading this book because recruiting salespeople is one of the hardest jobs to do.

Here is an example of one client we're working with now. He's a new leader who has quickly risen to national sales manager. And his story is very typical.

Straight away, he was expected to hire new salespeople. Cost was the most important thing. It didn't work. He struggled to attract quality candidates. He didn't have the time to understand who applied, and he struggled to get the time to interview.

When he did interviews, he realised that he wasn't attracting the right people.

When you're juggling too many balls and trying to manage a new team and grow, this is where you can outsource to external companies.

I don't classify us as a typical, traditional recruiter. We're a performance growth company that helps sales teams grow and scale their business. We don't just hire and run away. We are with our clients for the long haul.

"Every hire must be better than your last."
That's our motto.

We're heading into a new era of recruitment. AI is really impacting everyone, in both good and bad ways.

This might shock you, but I don't really look at resumes a lot. AI is now writing a lot of cover letters and resumes. That's why you need more than just a resume. I look at LinkedIn more than resumes.

When we're recruiting, we can attract over 200 applications. We then narrow that down quickly by using technology to uncover who are the best candidates. We also use AI outreach programs to contact great salespeople who aren't even looking for a new role. We utilise technology to bring the best people to the recruitment table. But this is only the start of our process.

This book also talks about the importance of retaining top sales talent. Not only is it very difficult to find quality talent, but it's also very easy to lose them if you're not doing the right thing. Maybe it's not giving them some flexibility in their life, if it's required. Or not paying the right money or not paying incentives (the biggest issue).

This book will show how to both attract and keep the top sales talent.

CHAPTER 1

Assessing Current Team Capabilities

If you're looking to recruit, it's always good to find out where you're at right now. We get contacted by leaders to help them recruit.

They're having trouble attracting the right person. But typically, they're also not growing, or winning any new business. Maybe they've tried to successfully launch new products and failed.

It's a very expensive exercise to add on another salesperson, particularly if you don't need them. It's about a return on investment.

CRYSTAL BALL RECRUITING

We're always happy to recruit for our clients, but more importantly, we want you to invest your money wisely.

I'll share a quick story with you about a company we worked with years ago—a sales team of approximately eight people.

The salespeople were typically hired for industry experience alone, and some worked within the business and then been given an opportunity to move into an external role.

It always sounds exciting for a salesperson to move into an external role. You get the car, you get a bit more status, you get the money, you get the freedom. There's a lot that goes with it.

At least half of the people in this company should never have been hired.

They were fish out of water in sales. The tough calls should have been made prior to the sales training program; it would have saved a lot of money training team members who weren't a good fit and who left during their training.

Once we built sales systems and processes for the company, it showed up the problems immediately.

Put it this way, if you remove your worst performers, it typically funds the investment of team training, evaluating your people, systems and process. Get this right, then train, coach, then recruit if still required. You'll be razor-focused on the gaps you need to fill, and the type of salespeople you require.

ASSESSING CURRENT TEAM CAPABILITIES

We also went on to hire three new sales guns—high level BDMs who have come out of the blocks as top performers.

Here are a few quick questions to answer about your business:

- Who's on your bus?
- How many salespeople do you actually need?
- Are they the right people to be on your bus?
- Are they in the right role?

Some businesses originally recruited for account management or customer service roles to look after and maintain what they've already got.

But their market has changed, and the pressure's now mounting.

They want to grow, but their costs have increased, and they need to increase sales. Sound familiar?

This is where it becomes very challenging. If you have the right people and they're in the right role, do they have a clear runway for what they should be doing? Or are they caught up in non-productive or non-related sales activities? That isn't always the salesperson's fault.

Sit with your team in your weekly 1:1's on Friday afternoon and open their calendars. Do they have scheduled meetings and a well-defined plan for the week? A lot of salespeople will wing it with no plan, doing more reactive selling instead.

That was a huge part of what I expected of my past sales managers—to make sure that their team had scheduled weekly meetings and plans in their calendars. That they knew who they would be seeing, and that they were seeing them at the right frequency and for the right reasons.

Some of us were lucky and we've had great mentors and managers, and we've learned to be able to do this and we can now share that with the salespeople we manage.

But if you come across a sales manager who hasn't had that managerial or mentoring experience, then potentially they're going to be a disaster at coaching somebody else because that's not how they work themselves.

Defining and Targeting Your Dream Clients

If you look at your sales pipeline (or hit list as we used to call it):

- Are your salespeople targeting the right types of prospects?
- Do they even understand what a good prospect looks like? We call it an ideal client profile (ICP). It's one of the biggest game-changers in new business development.
- Are your salespeople getting to the decision-makers?
- Can they have a conversation with the decision-maker at the right level? For example, C-suite, GM-level?

- Is it full of opportunities that your sales team can close?

A lot of salespeople can only get so far. Part of the issue why your business potentially may not be able to win dream clients is because your salespeople can only win what I call the 'low-hanging fruit'. For example, you could have a supply issue in your market which means someone has to come to you to buy. There's urgency and they order quickly.

But to win multiple dream clients, you need a problem to solve, and you need the right salespeople. Winning ongoing business is gold—the repetition after you've won the contract for a segment or a product category. And the orders keep rolling in, you don't have to fight for them.

We tend to find that there could be excuses why you will never win dream clients. It could be the strength of a competitor. Maybe they've been with them for years, and you don't want to rattle the cage.

But markets change. Product quality can vary. Is your strategy clear and current for today?

It's easy for salespeople to operate in reactive mode. They wake up each day, they're in the office, checking emails, and they're comfortable doing it. They're in reactive, customer-service mode.

I look back to when I was on the road myself. It's comfy and easy to see the clients you like. And, on reflection, you will avoid the ones that are tougher to win. I remember this well.

But they are key areas we need to look at when we're talking about your teams' current capabilities. For example, are incentives driving new business for you, or do they hinder it?

We see a lot of incentive programs that are out of date, and sometimes, there's no incentive program at all. We'll work on incentive programs later in the book.

My opinion based on years of managing and growing national sales teams is that if you want salespeople to target and win new business, then you need to provide incentives. Not everyone is motivated by money. We can also provide options for other types of incentives.

Start with identifying the dream clients you want, who is going to be able to deliver them for you, and what it will take to make that happen.

In addition, if your team has been neglected, if it's had no investment in training and development, if you haven't invested in technology and you've really run it into the ground, then you could be only running on a few cylinders. If you want to make a return on investment, then the party must be over.

Prevent Costly Repairs — Inspect Before You Invest

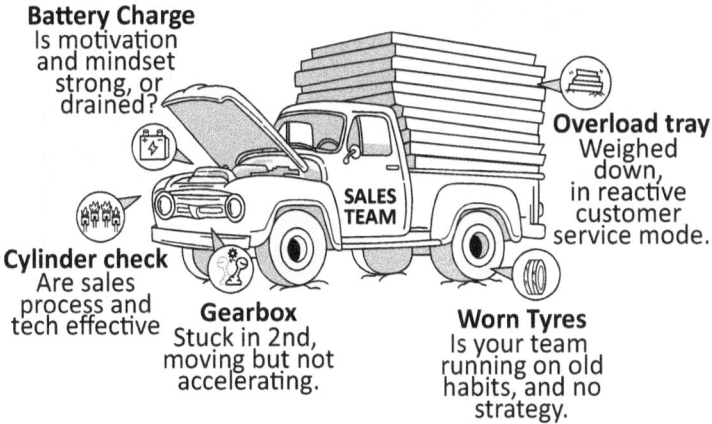

Battery Charge
Is motivation and mindset strong, or drained?

Overload tray
Weighed down, in reactive customer service mode.

SALES TEAM

Cylinder check
Are sales process and tech effective

Gearbox
Stuck in 2nd, moving but not accelerating.

Worn Tyres
Is your team running on old habits, and no strategy.

We can not only help you to recruit and retain top sales talent, but also to build effective and automated sales systems and processes.

If growth is your priority, and you've only got order-takers or account managers who are more service-oriented and reactive, then they won't take you to the next level to win your dream clients.

With some clients, we've helped to build a career trajectory from internal sales to an account management role, potentially then into a business development role of hunting. Then finally moving into sales management if they are a strong leader.

Your business will continue to struggle if you take the alternative approach of whacking someone straight into one of the hardest roles in one of the hardest markets with strong competitors.

The quicker you can get the right people in the right roles, then the sooner we can get your business out of second gear.

Here's another key question—are your high-performers typically undervalued and underinvested in?

I said this to a leader one day—what if your best salesperson was 10%-20% better?
He said it would be a game-changer.

Most of us focus on underperformance, but how can we get your best people even better and winning more new business? They deserve more investment.

Some companies are like a revolving door and frequently churn the bottom end of their sales team. Is there a pattern there? Are certain people getting all the good customers and the new people just expected to turn up and somehow win new work? Are they as good as you think they are?

The Cost of a Wrong Hire

At a $200,000 total investment per person (a realistic salesperson investment), are your current salespeople maximising their time effectively?

Right now, reducing business costs isn't easy. If your sales are down and your margins are down, instead of rushing to advertise for a new salesperson, we've had great success in investing the money saved into training our clients' existing sales team and investing in their automation technology and sales effectiveness instead.

We can look at your sales cycles. You can't supply the world, so let's get your team focused in the right areas:

- What is your niche?
- Who do you do well with? Why?
- Who else looks like them?

Because in a lot of situations, salespeople are comfortable to drive hundreds of kilometres, without an appointment, just to walk in and tell somebody how they are going.

"Are you okay?"

"Yes, thank you."

"See you next month."

"Right."

Now, I'm talking about a regional call here, and I've got one client of mine that I've been dealing with for over 20 years. He's a buyer. He runs when most salespeople come in.

He says to me, "I run and hide, because they don't offer me any value. And he's a big fella, so it's not easy for me to hide."

If You're Not Helping, You're Interrupting

"They waste my time. They're there just to say hello, to talk crap, right? I want people who are going to add value to my business."

Just having an account manager out there in case something happens isn't always a great way to work. In the future, I see less salespeople, but they've got to be better.

Think about 10-pin bowling when you put the barriers up. If you've got kids, you'll understand because you don't want their ball to go in the gutter. The barriers keep the ball going toward the pins.

You need to provide similar support for your salespeople to get consistent performance. Don't just trust that they know what to do and leave them alone to do it.

What we don't want to do is solely hire for industry experience. Everyone is doing it; the talent pool is low. Most have worked across multiple suppliers and you're going to pay more and you're potentially going to get somebody else's underperformer.

And the other thing we want to avoid is just focusing on hiring salespeople who have worked in successful companies. No matter who was in that job, they were going to succeed anyway. Maybe they had all the good accounts, or the business came to them.

If you're looking for a person to come in and win new business, well, that's a whole new level:

- We want salespeople who can focus on building a pipeline.
- We want the salespeople who will ask the hard questions. They're not worried about whether the customer likes them.
- We want the salesperson who is investing in using our technology and CRM (customer relationship management) system, logging calls, planning and targeting.
- We don't want the salespeople who are not even interested in winning any business. They're comfortable and we see that a lot. They should be knowing where they're going, who they're seeing, who they're targeting, and where that target is at.

Sales is like sport. You need to build muscle, and you need to keep learning and push the boundaries. You need to train, and I'm not talking about every 10 years, right?

I'm talking about training every day, every week, every month, every year.

You need to try a new set play via processes you can build, otherwise you're going to get left behind because your competitors will be doing it.

You must have your best team on the ground. Now, if we find that some salespeople avoid tech, then it's a problem to scale your business. If you're leveraging technology, they need to be able to use it.

Similarly, if you're head-hunting for experience and you want to get them on your team, then don't accept excuses for non-compliance with daily sales activity. Don't let them do whatever they want. I've seen that approach fail many times. It never works, and their attitude will rub off on the rest of your team.

You can download more information by visiting:www. jasonhowes.com.au/books/downloads.

CHAPTER 2

Making an ROI on Your Salespeople

Sales requires passion to succeed. Some people have it, some don't. It's also possible someone you hired years ago did a strong desire, but has lost it.

A high percentage of hiring managers don't know what their ROI (return on investment) is on their salespeople. I was the same. None of us have ever been taught. Technology has helped us to better understand this, but many companies haven't been set up to use it the right way.

We dig deep into the areas that can help support sales growth and deliver an ROI. The example I quite often use is this—when you've hired someone, imagine watching them drive down the road with the window down and $100 notes flying out.

Every kilometre can cost you money. If you've got a lot of salespeople out there not being managed, or not knowing your costs, then it will eat into your profits.

For example, quite often we see a company headhunt someone from their competitor. They pay top dollar, only to find out that they're an average salesperson at best. I've done it myself in the past.

You're now stuck with a high base and high cost. You realise that you're in trouble.

Long term, it isn't sustainable and from a performance perspective, we're seeing this now with a lot of redundancies, a lot of restructures and increased organisational realignment. An increasing number of companies are simply not making enough money.

Recruitment moves very fast and changes quickly. As an executive sales coach and recruiter, we get daily calls from sales professionals who have been made redundant. Many know they're not going to get the same money again.

They were being overpaid and sucking up company profits, but to be fair, they were overpaid by inexperienced hiring managers.

We also speak with some amazing candidates who are worthy of a high dollar investment, but they tend to be the ones you won't see.

But if the wrong person is hired and you've paid too much, then you have a BIG problem.

That's why we bring in the experts to conduct a "sales DNA assessment"[4] before we hire, irrespective of someone's experience and where they've worked because we want to make sure they're aligned to the role.

Imagine finding out before you invest your valuable time in interviewing whether a person is a good fit, has a strong mindset, is coachable and can sell.

In-House Recruitment Cost Breakdown

This table outlines the typical costs associated with recruiting a new team member in-house. It includes interview expenses, reference checks and onboarding costs, and it highlights the potential disruption to business operations.

In-House Recruitment Cost Breakdown

Item	Time	Summary	Cost
Job Preperation	2 hours	Review Past success	$ 1,000
Job advert	2 hours	Write + Cost advert	$ 1,000
Screen Candidates	5 hours	Review shortlist	$ 2,000
First Interview	5 hours * 2 people	5 to 10 candidates	$ 1,500
Second Interview	5 hours * 2 people	3 to 5 candidates	$ 1,500
Reference Checks	1 hour	Background verification	$ 500
Medical & Police	1 hour	Complience Checks	$ 500
Cost to Hire	21 hours	Min Cost to Hire	$ 8,000 AUD

The hidden price tag of hiring mistakes
3,6 or 12 months later

Onboarding (3 Months)	Salary, car, tools of trade	3 Months	$ 45,000+$ 8,000
Onboarding (6 Months)	Salary, car, tools of trade	6 Months	$ 90,000+$ 8,000
Onboarding (12 Months)	Salary, car, tools of trade	12 Months	$ 180,000+$ 8,000
Cost per Hire	"Example"	6 Months	$ 98,000

*Disruption to your business
and clients: priceless.*

Our Recruitment Outsourcing Value Alternative

We have clients where we've replaced 80% of their sales team with people who can sell. We were called in initially because of these clients' lack of sales. We were bought in to remove the responsibility from hiring managers who weren't skilled in recruiting.

That's why we've written this book. Our priority is to get better salespeople in your business.

Many of the other tasks of a sales manager can be burdened by having to hire. It's time consuming. It's a pain.

There's a lot of false starts. Hire, fail, rehire, fail is not uncommon.

A lot of clients who contact us are initially frustrated. Many feel trapped. And they've been hurt by recruiters, like I was when I was a hiring manager. They were simply thrown candidates with industry experience by external recruitment companies. Anyone with a pulse... who moved and turned up.

They would fail, then be replaced as per the agreement by another salesperson with industry experience, who would fail, and it was going around like a hamster wheel.

At some point, these leaders needed to eat humble pie, and that is the investment to get better salespeople. And for us to prove the value of working with us.

Our experience and specialty in training, coaching, and recruitment provides areas of improvement for our clients.

We have a lot more buy-in than other recruiters. We're always committed to the long game. We have confidence that our candidates will last longer, because we remove major barriers by not hiring the bottom half of salespeople when they're assessed using the sales DNA assessment.

We won't just put people forward unless we've got the data to back them up.

If you're interested in what I'm talking about here, maybe you're in the middle of recruiting someone now and you're down to a shortlist, then as a token of our appreciation for reading our book, we're offering you 15% off your first sales DNA assessment.

If you've got candidates in your pool, we'll put them through and have results within 24 hours.

If they're recommended, that's great for you, if they're not, well then, we've saved you a big headache, not only now, but down the track when you're trying to performance-manage this person. And spending $200 k! This is the best investment you'll make!

Think about it as a tool for your sales toolbox to enable you to recruit with more confidence and science.

Now, we have a few gaps that we tend to identify when we're looking to help leaders hire.

If you're looking for a return on your investment:

- Are your current compensation plans motivating the right behaviours? That's one of the big questions that we ask, because if it's not, well then something needs to change.
- Can your team explain how they earn their incentives quite easily? They should be able to do this. Within a few minutes. It should be an easy yes.

New hires have the right to see this if they're signing a contract. Have it ready to go, so there's no hidden surprises down the track for either of you. Be transparent.

When you are hiring, are you attracting and keeping quality sales hunters? This is where you need objective data to guide your hiring and performance decisions.

And are you confident your sales hires are going to deliver a 3x to 5x return on investment?

If you're unsure about any of these questions, then it's time to take a closer look.

Understanding ROI Benchmarks for Sales Incentives

Our approach leverages market data across both low-sales/high-margin and high-sales/low-margin scenarios, recognising that our clients operate across a spectrum of business models. The impact of these variables is significant when determining how best to reward salespeople.

We provide 3x and 5x ROI benchmarks, grounded in industry best practices. These benchmarks are designed to be adjustable and can be tailored to suit your business, product mix and margin profile. An example 5x ROI is provided below.

How to Calculate Your ROI and Maximise Your Investment

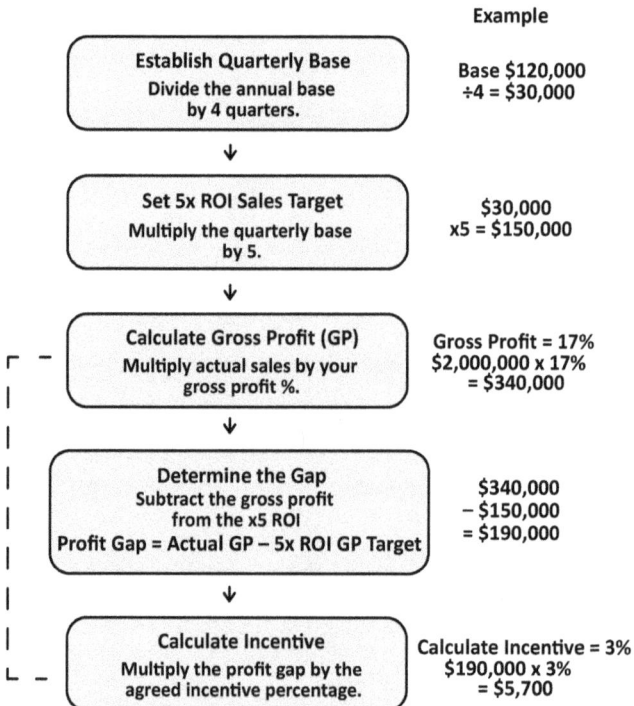

Example

Establish Quarterly Base
Divide the annual base by 4 quarters.

Base $120,000
÷4 = $30,000

↓

Set 5x ROI Sales Target
Multiply the quarterly base by 5.

$30,000
x5 = $150,000

↓

Calculate Gross Profit (GP)
Multiply actual sales by your gross profit %.

Gross Profit = 17%
$2,000,000 x 17%
= $340,000

↓

Determine the Gap
Subtract the gross profit from the x5 ROI
Profit Gap = Actual GP – 5x ROI GP Target

$340,000
– $150,000
= $190,000

↓

Calculate Incentive
Multiply the profit gap by the agreed incentive percentage.

Calculate Incentive = 3%
$190,000 x 3%
= $5,700

Accounting for Costs and New Hires

It is crucial to fully understand your costs, particularly when considering new hires. Factoring in a ramp-up period is essential, as it is unrealistic to expect new employees to immediately start earning incentives within the first three, six, nine or even twelve months. The specifics depend on your sales cycle and how you choose to structure key performance levers within the role.

From a personal perspective, ensuring that new hires are meeting critical success criteria provides leverage. If they are not performing as required, their rewards can be withheld. This complexity makes it worthwhile to invest time in understanding the true costs and ROI of your sales team, especially as recruitment costs rise and quality candidates become harder to source.

Scenarios

- **Low Sales Volume, Mid-Level Margin**
  For clients in wholesale, manufacturing, trade and retail, margins and volumes can vary significantly. For example, with a sales budget of $400,000 per month and a 25% gross profit margin, the required profit is $100,000. If the 3x base cost for an account manager is $67,750, there remains a $22,250 profit gap. A 5% incentive paid on this gap equates to $1,062.50 per quarter, or $354.20 per month. It is important to assess whether this structure is sustainable for

the business and sufficiently rewarding for the salesperson. If not, triggers may need to be adjusted to ensure all parties benefit.

- **Increasing Sales Targets**
  Raising the sales budget to $550,000 , at the same margin yields $137,500 profit. After accounting for a 3x base ($67,750) the gap increases to $70,000. At a 5% profit share, this translates to $3,500 per quarter or $1,166.67 per month. Higher sales targets provide greater profit gaps and, consequently, more attractive incentives for salespeople. Adjustments to sales volume or margin can further enhance the benefits.

- **High-Margin Scenario**
  For companies with high margins, such as those in manufacturing, the incentive structure may differ. For example, with a $600,000 budget and a 40% gross profit margin, the profit is $240,000. Removing the 3x base ($90,000) leaves a $150,000 profit gap. A 5% profit share provides $7,500 per quarter. The amount shared is at the business owner's discretion and should be revisited if capacity or ownership changes occur. Including relevant clauses or appendices in contracts ensures flexibility in the event of mergers or unforeseen industry changes.

  Using the same $600,000 budget and 40% gross profit, a 5x ROI equates to $150,000 (five times a $30,000 base). The resulting profit gap is $90,000, and a 5% commission paid on this gap amounts to $4,500 per quarter. Businesses can choose between 3x or 5x ROI benchmarks to suit their specific goals and circumstances, with all structures fully customisable.

Evaluating Compensation Plans

It is essential to evaluate whether your current compensation plans drive performance, offer predictability and scalability, and motivate the right behaviours. If your organisation is not currently paying out incentives, it may be time to reconsider your approach. Techniques such as multipliers or interim adjustments can stimulate sales activity while ensuring both business profitability and salesperson opportunity.

Be cautious when scaling production with high sales and low margins, as this can impact profitability. Balancing growth with profitability is key.

Commission structures should always be documented separately and reviewed regularly to accommodate changes in business circumstances.

HR Support and Documentation

To assist with documentation and HR support, a free consultation and discount is available, on request. Proper documentation can prevent costly disputes over commissions, which are often sensitive topics.

We have an ROI white paper available for business leaders, HR managers and sales leaders. It provides a detailed report and examples for making an ROI on your salespeople. You can download it at www.jasonhowes.com.au/books/downloads.

Checklist

Here is a quick checklist for business leaders:

- **If your salespeople have a high base, they might be too comfortable.**

Some baby boomers or even Gen X may be winding down, focused more on lifestyle than growth. That's fine—but does it align with your strategy?

- **Sometimes, someone with a mortgage and bills to pay is more driven to chase business.**

But many teams lack incentives to spark new business development. Is your current setup motivating growth—or making it easy to stay in a comfort zone? It's common for reps to get stuck in customer service, emails, and familiar clients—avoiding the ones who could bring in new business.

Sometimes, all salespeople in a business are paid the same, regardless of experience.

Personally, I don't agree with it, but I understand why some companies want to level out the base salaries and then offer the opportunity to earn more on incentives. But again, everyone has different experience and motivation, and what we find is that when one salesperson leaves, the customers are up for grabs before you advertise for the next salesperson. It's like a dogfight for a bone. I've been there... It's ugly ☹.

And if someone gets all the good customers, then they could end up earning some attractive incentives, which are incentives based on your business success, not necessarily what they've done to maintain or grow the customer. That creates a comfortable environment.

- **Sometimes, underperformers are paid too much and high performers not enough.**

Again, pulling back the covers, who are the top performers in your business?

And who are the ones just cruising along and not actually adding to your new business results and success?

The best investment you can make to start with is a sales DNA assessment to uncover your salespeople, systems, and processes.

Chapter 5 talks in detail about how to make a 3x to 5x ROI. It's so important to understand your costs. It's quite complex but it's worth your time to understand your costs and return on investment for your sales team.

Sometimes we build tiered interim targets. Or add in accelerators/multipliers for a guaranteed percentage ROI within the first six months. This can help. Plug in leading KPIs (key performance indicators) that will move the needle. Reward your team for small wins to build their confidence. Bringing someone straight in off the street and paying them a high incentive program is not going to help anyone.

Here's a quick recruitment story.

A past client of mine was a very aggressive selling company in the timber industry. They bought hard and they sold hard. The owner, let's say his name is Ken, called me one day and he said, "Jase, I've got one question for you. We've got a guy interviewed for the job. You know him. Can he sell or NOT? I'm not here to mess around."

My answer? "No."

He wasn't an aggressive salesperson. He wouldn't have lasted, so I did him a favour anyway.

New business development is a hunting role. These recruits are expected to generate a return on investment. Sometimes we need to ask people hard questions when we're hiring:

- Are you confident?
- Are you capable of doing this job?
- Will you consistently hunt for new business every day?

MAKING AN ROI ON YOUR SALESPEOPLE

You want this person to earn the right to work at your company. Don't just hire for industry experience or because they're likeable or they're available now. Sales is a hard grind.

With sales targets, don't just hand over half of your business and then reward someone for just doing their job. If you want to get a return on investment, make them earn their stripes. I know I did. It makes you appreciate the wins, and losses much more.

And make sure you reward for margin. If someone's selling at a higher margin, then consider uncapped incentives, or even capped incentives, but never allow your salespeople to set the pricing. The number one reason that you could go broke is if you let your salespeople do the pricing.

If you buy better or purchase more competitively, if there's a change in the currency, or if there's a shortage and you can sell for more, then do it.

Don't give your salesperson the right to sell what they want to because they will go cost plus. I've seen it many times. Your need to work from the market rate backwards. Reverse engineer. What's the best price we can get? Sell for more margin. Reward them for selling value, not just price.

It's quite contagious when your salespeople win and they start to earn more. They'll build confidence.

You'll see it change the conversations. I always used to know if I was dealing with a procurement manager who just worked for the company, it's a completely different story to dealing with someone who owns the business.

You want your salespeople to sell like they own your business. It will give you a better return on investment every time, guaranteed.

Ensure that your incentive program is easy to follow. It should be able to read on the back of a coaster or cocktail napkin.

Remove obstacles for your salespeople. Give them a clear run at sales growth. If they divert back to comfort mode, then you've got a problem.

And regularly go back to their position description. Make sure they're doing the job they are supposed to be doing. Ensure they're clear on who to target.

Start them off with a strong onboarding program (see Chapter 8). Get them a buddy. Make sure it's a good one who's succeeded themselves.

Get the right people in the right role and have a sales process that works that they can follow, and that you can scale from. It's a game-changer.

And make sure you coach your people. Don't just let them be, most need guidance. Have your weekly 1:1's. They only need to be for 15 minutes, but then follow up, follow up, and follow up. Integrate technology to make it more efficient.

What would it mean to your business if your high performers were 10% better? The results will pay for themselves.

Underperformers typically get more time from leaders than overperformers. Can you get your bottom 50% of salespeople into your top 30% by investing in their professional development? Coach them up or coach them out.

Underperformers must go, but make sure you get a sales DNA assessment before they go. Sometimes I've seen it where you can move someone on and then the next person comes and they are worse.

I say this to leaders we're working with: "Remove your worst performer, and invest that money into working with us to help you build a high-performance sales team before you rush to hire and get somebody else who's potentially just as bad." Pause and reflect.

Your business should be like a well-oiled machine. You should know your outputs, stats, win-loss ratio, sales cycle length, and why you're losing opportunities.

There are too many times that we see someone get hired and the leader or hiring manager is expecting them to fix all their problems. It's not going to happen.

CHAPTER 3

Clearly Defining the Role

It's always good to reflect at this stage:

- What percentage of your sales team turns over each year?
- What percentage are hitting target?
- When did you last update the PD (position description) you're hiring for? Most companies we start working with don't have current and accurate precision descriptions.

It's critical that you open the gate to attracting and hiring from a wider talent pool.

If you're a sales leader, you might need to replace somebody who has resigned, or you need to add a new sales performer.

Maybe you're looking to turn the business around. I've been in your shoes. It's not easy, and there's a lot of work we can do before you start searching.

I'll share a little sales story with you about a client we worked with many years ago. When we came in to work with the business, people were being pulled from pillar to post, but don't be alarmed.

This client's business was quite mature. It had grown a lot over the years and was once very innovative, but they had lost their way. Unfortunately, there was no new business coming in, and there was business being lost out the back end to competitors.

The business owner wanted to grow, but the people that he had on his team couldn't do it and didn't want to. When I started to ask questions about what their BDMs were doing, the feedback was from his manager that they were always in the office.

If you're a salesperson going into the office every day and doing customer service inquiries and activities, then you're not a business development manager. Let's just call out the elephant in the room. You're an internal salesperson.

You're overpaid, and someone should have made a call on you a long time ago.

When we said, "Okay, let's get this person back in the field," the response was, "They don't know where to go. They don't know who to see."

Now, for me, that's quite an unusual response. I couldn't believe it.

I was asked to build a call planner to help them. I got paid a small fortune to do a simple job. I asked simple questions:

- Who are they currently dealing with?
- Where are their sales at now?
- Where were their sales at?
- Who are they not dealing with?
- Who did they lose?
- Where's the opportunities for new business?

Then I started to map out a core planner. I shouldn't have been doing it. Had I been working with them earlier, I would have moved the person on a long time before that. Let's just say they didn't last long after this.

Promoting the Right Behaviours and Expectations

Your PD needs to define the role with the right numbers and right activities to be successful. Then we can find the most suitable candidate.

This will also help you understand how to manage your current team members if they are underperforming compared to the newly defined role requirements.

The PD will help you successfully onboard new salespeople. I'll talk more about onboarding in Chapter 8.

Together, if required, we build the systems and processes, then we get it to work with automation. Repetition that works. This is the beauty of scaling a sales team. It will also improve team engagement and provide clearer development opportunities.

If someone does leave, you have their role defined, along with systems and processes. You know what you're looking for and it gives you the ability to be able to recruit that person much more effectively. The process becomes very easy to follow.

For example, if a company wants more new sales, which is where we specialise, then we need to be more focussed on removing the daily noise that stops them from working in comfortable areas like customer service-related activities.

It's so common for us to see salespeople caught up in the wrong activities. Sometimes it's not all their fault, sometimes it is. It could be that companies are reducing headcount now and they're looking to stretch people to cover multiple roles. Most people are now doing a role and a bit in this current market. Money is tight.

I understand why that's happening, but it's not going to help grow sales if the salesperson also has to do the marketing or customer service or whatever else on the side and still be expected to hit targets. Something will give.

Ten Questions to Ensure the Sales Role is Defined for Success

1. What is expected from your salesperson daily?
2. Are they in the field three or four days a week?
3. Are they seeing existing customers daily?
4. How many calls a day are they doing?
5. What is the mix of existing sales to the required number of new sales calls.
6. What activities will drive new business opportunities?
7. How many booked meetings with new prospects do you expect?
8. How many new prospect opportunities should be in your pipeline?
9. What accounts need to be won or reactivated?
10. What leading KPIs will drive effectiveness?

CRYSTAL BALL RECRUITING

Leading KPIs

1 Quota: Achieve $2M in new business within the first 12 months.

2 Pipeline Development: Identify 10 new commercial buildings per month that require fiber optic cable, and 2 potential anchor accounts in each building, for a total of 20 potential accounts. Have 5 meetings a week with the facility manager, IT Director, or COO of those 20 accounts

3 Conversion Rate: Convert 40% of meetings = 2 qualified proposals weekly for 8/month.

4 Close Rate: Close 25% of proposals = acquire 2 new anchor accounts (contracts) per month with a minimum contract value of $10,000/month each.

5 Client Retention: Achieve and maintain a client retention rate of 90% or higher through personalized engagement. Requires an NPS between 50 and 70, which is classified as excellent.

6 Sales Cycle Optimization: Reduce the sales cycle from 90 days to 60 days by meeting with all the decision-makers.

7 CRM: Achieving 100% CRM utilization is crucial for enhancing sales results and improving effectiveness

8 Pipeline Metrics (30/60/90 Days after 3 months ramp up):
30 days: 20 meetings, 8 proposals, 2 deals ($10K each)
60 days: 40 meetings, 16 proposals, 4 deals ($10K each)
90 days: 60 meetings, 24 proposals, 6 deals ($10K each)

These are key metrics that we can start to talk about to really break down what's important for your business right now to get the wheels moving. Leading KPIs should drive your incentive program.

A PD sets your expectations. And with salespeople, we need to draw the line in the sand, and you need to be very firm. I know, I've been there. It's like herding cats! Set clear expectations, and don't let go. You want to be fair and reasonable, but the basics need to be achieved because the basics will combine and contribute to the big wins within the business that you need.

Using CRM Automation

Technology has come a long way, and with AI it is flying. We build out a lot of processes, systems and KPIs so that salespeople can use automation, like using voice to text. We show them how it will save them time, make them more effective, and that it provides value for them to use it daily.

Technology should help people, not hinder them. When you're defining the role, you set the expectations, and the salesperson signs off on it. Using tech is part of the sales job. I always used to say to my salespeople that if you want to get paid, then we expect you to use the tools. Get group buy-in as a sales team.

Leadership has its own responsibilities as well. You MUST take ownership of all your data. You should be able to click in at any time of the day and see who's doing what, where they are at, and how you can help them.

One of the big areas to focus on is ensuring that your sales team's activities are aligned with your business goals and strategy. It's very important to make sure everyone's on the same trajectory.

Sometimes, people are all over the place. I've seen this before working with clients. Their salespeople are chasing everything that they shouldn't be. It's about understanding where you're going because you want to be able to make sure that your arrow is aimed at your target, not relying on chance.

Many salespeople just hope that opportunities are going to fall into their lap. That can happen, as we saw during COVID with product shortages and issues with supply. Demand was seriously pulled forward. But a lot of those new customers, where are they now? Are they back dealing with your major competitor? Some are more cautious now, and their business may be split between a few suppliers.

What Does Success Look Like?

This is one of the greatest questions. The new person that I'm hiring or defining their role more clearly in my existing team looks like this:

- They're bringing in new opportunities and new clients.
- They're selling more effectively.
- They're successfully launching new product categories.
- They improve margin by selling value.
- They are consultative—asking good questions to uncover compelling reasons to change.
- They create urgency to get opportunities across the line and orders in hand.
- They update each sales call in the CRM immediately after each meeting, not later.

- They use marketing in their sales process to support and grow the brand.

I know as a sales leader, when someone brings you back an opportunity and asks, "Can you help me?", it's GOLD. Better than the person who never brings anything back, right?

Or better than the person that comes back and just wants a cheaper price to close. Price is not everything. Unfortunately, a lot of salespeople are taught to lead with price. So that's what success might look like instead. Somebody leading with value.

To build a high-performance sales team and culture takes a lot of planning and a lot of role- defining to make sure you get the right people in the right role doing the right activities on a consistent basis.

Role Titles

Let's have a talk about the importance of having the right or appropriate role title. I've worked with leaders that don't care about role titles. They're more flexible, but I've seen that approach backfire many times.

For example, a business development person was given the opportunity to pick a title, so they selected 'sales director'. Now, good on them, but the unfortunate part is the other salespeople in the business picked their own titles as well, and they had no reflection of this person having the title of sales director.

Or an account manager with a title of sales or State manager, when they're the only person in the State!

(Remember to cross-reference a candidate's resume with LinkedIn, sometimes you'll see they do not match. I prefer LinkedIn, it's live and more visible.)

You can see how these areas get a bit cloudy, but from my perspective, I agree that if you're actively prospecting, then a stronger title can potentially open more doors for you.

If you're trying to get in to see a CEO, and not being disrespectful here as I've been an account manager, but you're probably going to struggle to get a meeting as an account manager. You'll be directed down to a relevant level.

But if you've got the title of business development manager or sales manager, then you have more chance of getting in the door. If you do, you've still got to be able to 'talk the talk' though, right? That's why salespeople will sometimes leverage a senior manager or their CEO to attend with them. I used to do this quite often when required.

And again, that's a whole new level of dealing with people at C-suite or national procurement level, where it's common they get bombarded with meeting requests.

A sales executive or account executive is quite a good title, but it doesn't drill into the priority of the role. In theory, this could be more of an account management role. An account manager or sales rep might be the best title choice if your business is more established. The salesperson could be managing a territory or a segment. If so, add that. Keep it simple. For example, BDM—Commercial, BDM—Residential.

If you have international influence, then you will likely find vice president or president more common than sales manager or national sales manager.

ROLE	PRIMARY FOCUS	COMMON PITFALLS
Internal Sales / Customer Success	Retention, service and inbound orders	Overlooked as a growth engine, limited incentives
Sales Development Representative	Cold outreach, qualifying leads	Promoted too early without performance track records
Sales Representative	Territory sales, mix of service and growth	Jack/jill-of-all-trades roles dilute focus
Technical Sales Representative	Solutions-led sales with deep product knowledge	Hired for technical skill, not sales capability
Account Manager	Maintain and grow current clients	Misaligned compensation for new business initiatives
AM/BDM Hybrid	Blend of farming and hunting	Lack of clarity on expectations or targets
Business Development Manager	Win new business, new markets	Never trained, need prospecting support
Key Account Manager	Grow large strategic clients	Lack of differentiation from standard AMs
Regional Sales Manager	Lead teams across a region	Poor coaching and role overload
Sales Manager	Coach, forecast and develop salespeople	Carrying their own patch instead of leading, not trained to coach
National Sales Manager	Drive strategy and national team performance	Spread too thin across pricing, ops, sales and strategy
GM of Sales	Set vision and lead go-to-market execution	Misaligned KPIs, stuck in operational weeds

If you have 10 salespeople, there's probably only one or two that are going to be able to successfully create and win new business opportunities. That's the sort of numbers you're looking at.

So, how many are in your team?

How many bring new opportunities to the table?

And what percentage of that is your sales team?

If you're talking about a sales manager role, then a title that's being used a lot of the moment is head of sales. Another one could be head of growth. That one is great if your strategy is to scale. New products, new segments, new industries. It's a growth role; it's not just sales.

Quick Tip: Go with the title that most reflects what the salesperson is doing. If it is more hunting, then 'business development manager' is a good choice.

Some companies don't want the 'manager' word in the title because sometimes it can push the salary up. Business development representative is an alternative.

I also like companies that allow for a vision. We quite often build a sales career trajectory with them. If a salesperson is performing and can see opportunities for career progression, which a lot of top salespeople want now, then they only move up if they earn their stripes.

They could start as an account manager or sales representative. If they do well there, they move into a business development manager role. If you do well there, they move into regional or State sales management. If they do well there, they can move into national sales management.

Setting up a career trajectory also gives you the ability to reward based on performance and what they've contributed to the business. But remember, don't expect them to move through the ranks without investing in their professional development. Find a good mentor or sales coach to support them and ramp them up quicker. It's a wise investment to ensure success.

Another emerging trend now is SDR—sales development rep. I see more of this in the future. If you've got an internal person that's showing some signs of wanting to really go to the next level in sales, you can make them a sales development rep. It's an internal position, so you don't need to give them a car. This role is focused on winning new business with smaller accounts that don't require a sales rep to visit. Having this role reduces the cost of running around the countryside with fuel and accommodation. (A CRM and effective sales process can help to manage these accounts and ensure transparency between your team members.)

An SDR role could be a good choice if your business is more established and you're limited in terms of products to grow your market share. The core responsibility is to service current accounts and ensure sales are maintained, but there is also a good opportunity to win new business and see if they have the ability to do that. It's a good grooming role for an external sales position.

But again, lead with caution. Not everyone is cut out for external sales.

Our recommendation always is to do a sales DNA assessment.[5] It helps you to ensure they're cut out for sales, and you can use it for onboarding, training and coaching. And you get to pick the most suitable person for the role if you have multiple people put up their hands. Without bias.

The sales DNA assessment will provide you with predictive and accurate data on whether a person has the necessary desire and commitment. It will test their mindset, their motivation styles, and identify their current sales abilities and skill sets. In the long term, you're doing them a favour because I've seen it before where people are pushed out into the field and they fail terribly. It's not always their fault. They were never meant to be in sales.

Using an objective assessment is a far better investment because you could lose a good internal person or someone within the business that was doing a good job, just because they wanted a car or they wanted more money or they wanted the status.

Get the right person for the right role. It pays off and makes your life much easier.

In larger geographic areas, some companies expect salespeople to manage, nurture and win new business. It doesn't make sense to send multiple people, but unfortunately a lot of salespeople really struggle to win new business. They become more like relationship managers with existing customers by ensuring service levels are achieved and sometimes managing inventory.

A hybrid account manager/BDM is ideal for geographic regions that require both maintenance and growth. I have seen companies have specialised BDMs within the metropolitan market where the volume is and then the account manager/ BDM hybrid role to cover country or regional locations.

Once again, the specifics of a role must be identified in its position description, so everyone knows that you want to both hold business and grow your market share. You don't want to get someone who's not going to want to grow market share, if that's your strategy.

It's a little bit like finding an all-rounder in cricket. It's very uncommon to find someone who can bat and bowl, right? But the good thing is, if you've got someone that can bat and you want them to bowl as well, we can train for performance improvement.

We've helped many salespeople become more skilled in winning new business by understanding and overcoming some of the mindset and tactical barriers that they have. And we find this investment pays off very quickly. It pays for itself.

But be aware that the hybrid role isn't easy. 70% of the companies that we hire for want business development managers because they want help in creating, progressing and closing new business. It's a tough area to succeed in, but it's our passion.

Whether it involves winning new customers or selling new products and new categories to existing customers, recruiting and developing sales hunters is our specialty.

Sales hunting is an art that right now probably only 10 to 15% of salespeople can do successfully.

Salespeople are not born. They're made.

Most salespeople have never had any training or development. Potentially, you could have some good people within your business now. And potentially, you don't need to hire someone.

It could be better to remove one of your underperformers to fund a sales training, coaching program to get the most out of your better salespeople.

Our mission is to help you grow sales and do it effectively.

Sales Management

Sales managers are one of the key roles we recruit for, but most salespeople have never been trained in being a sales manager. Most of us were good at sales. We could have been a bit of a lone wolf. We've never been taught how to recruit for salespeople. We've never been taught how to manage a sales team.

Fortunately, some of us have had fantastic mentors. Peter Dallimore, Peter Hyne and John Andrew taught me what it was like to be managed by a professional person. They were all completely different, but the combination provided me with the tools to succeed.

Now, we all learn that we take the good, and we don't take the bad. It's about understanding what drives you as a manager.

One leader we worked with had eight salespeople. He was CEO and struggling. He'd hired the wrong people, had no tech, didn't have time to coach and he was losing market share. Unfortunately, he didn't want to make the hard calls and pushed back on change after he saw how much needed to change... That's not uncommon, when you're stuck in a rut.

If you're like anyone else, you're wearing multiple hats, and sales management is not your major priority. And I understand that because you're doing everything else.

So this is where we find there's a huge gap. A CEO typically doesn't have time.

We do a lot of work by coming in and helping our clients to understand where they're at and supporting their vision. To help them build and implement sales management systems and processes.

Sales managers shouldn't be managing direct accounts except for maybe some strategic key accounts. The sales manager's responsibility is to ensure that salespeople succeed in aligning sales strategy with marketing and overall business goals.

The role of the sales manager is to be out in the market, not doing 10,000 other things involved with operations, procurement and customer service that takes them away from their priority to manage sales, and to get the best out of their salespeople.

Coaching should be 50% of a sales manager's time.

I'll say that again. It's so important. If you're looking to hire a sales manager, 50% of their time should be on coaching their sales team to be successful. I really need to stress this.

Don't fall into the trap of promoting someone to the sales manager's role who's from internal or external sales or operations just because they want the money or the better car.

I've seen it first-hand; it will fail probably 80% of the time. Look, it could be a family member who needs a position of authority. I get it. But sales management is a critical role, they'll only coach and support your team effectively as they've been taught how to do it. With no experience, you're passing that down the line to your business and team. It will fail. Unless you train your sales manager by investing in their development. You need to support them to become more successful.

A national sales manager's job is very tough. I know, I did it for over 13 years.

They should be there to support the sales team. That's their priority. Don't force them to take on non-relevant activities, or roles they're not trained to do. A classic example is marketing.

It's not an easy seat to fill. I'm all about promoting from within companies, but get the best person for the role. Don't just put a person in the role because it's comfortable and you might only have needed to throw an extra five or 10 grand at them (and in many cases, get them to still do their current role).

It might seem like you're saving money. But trust me, it's *costing* you money. And at the end of the day, it'll only put pressure on everyone else if they don't perform. It's like finals footy. Every person in your team needs to deserve their role so you can win the big games.

If you don't have the right people in the right role, it's going to make it more challenging for you to win. Every person who isn't the right fit is going to put more weight on your shoulders.

Quick Position Description Tips:

- PDs are not 'set and forgets', they require ongoing maintenance to stay relevant.
- Clarity matters, make sure your PD is on point.
- Provide a clear line of sight to how each person contributes to your company's success.
- Clear goals will reduce frustration and turnover, so make sure your leaders are aligned.
- Remember what success looks like. Ensure this is front and centre in your PD.

CHAPTER 4

Compensation and Incentives

As a business leader, we want to make as much money as we can out of a salesperson. It's critical to know the compensation and incentives that will drive new business by motivating your sales team:

- How much can they earn?
- How can I maximise what they're earning?

It's a very important topic from a salesperson's point of view, number one. But not everyone is motivated by money.

One of the key criteria is to be aware of current compensation schemes and incentives in your industry.

We see it as our job to ensure your top performers are safe. But I've seen many companies simply overpay just to

65

protect their top performers from leaving, like a "knock-out bid" at an auction. No one can get close to it. It's too good for the top performer to leave.

But that also comes with risk. What if they get comfortable and lose motivation, riding on their past success with the top clients. What if they're no longer the person you originally hired? That's a potential trap if you are overpaying and they're cruising.

There's also a risk of you're not paying enough. A lot of companies contact us when they fear losing quality sales professionals to their opposition. If those people have been offered a great package and a role that ticks more boxes, then sometimes the horse has already bolted. It's too late.

I've had this situation myself. Many years ago, I was offered a 50% pay increase and it was too good to refuse. At that time, with a big reno happening, our beautiful first daughter was a toddler, and we had plans for our second. Money was king, and I needed it, so I took the opportunity. It ended up working for me in that situation.

But I look back and now I can see that money isn't everything. Culture is also very important. As a business, we receive over 5,000 applications each year. When we're recruiting for our clients, we've seen the impact that conversations can have, and it's rewarding when someone gets their dream job and more money.

That's why this chapter is quite long and detailed. It took me a while to put it together.

As I mentioned earlier in the book, from my personal experience in over 35 years of sales, not all salespeople should be paid the same. That's my opinion. We're all different.

Potentially, if you've managed major accounts and successfully won new business, then it is totally fair that you would want more. You back yourself and you know the value you bring to the table; you want to get rewarded for it.

But business costs are up and margins are down. Most businesses are under extreme pressure to reduce costs. And sometimes, if you're hiring a salesperson and you throw a cheap, low-ball number at them, then you might want to be a little bit concerned because potentially that's all they think they're worth. But it could be an easy-come, easy-go scenario if they have bills to pay.

Someone that is potentially further into their career, that's done well in property, and that has no debt (lucky them) may not be a good choice if your strategy is to scale and grow. It depends how they're motivated.

I worked with a salesperson years ago, and his partner earned a very good income. All he was worried about was a fair base and a car he could choose to suit his lifestyle. Money didn't motivate him. But our client wanted to grow sales. This salesperson wasn't motivated to do that. He was more about work/life balance.

Now, I understand that, but again, you really need to be clear on what you're looking for.

I like it when a younger salesperson wants to purchase a home (or just did) and they're keen to pay it off. Typically, they may have more motivation to chase money, to get ahead. More buy-in.

If they're more extrinsically driven, they want to earn more money. They want to buy nice things. They want to have the sports car. They will potentially chase commissions.

When I was leading a sales team, they were all on the same incentive system. Some people would chase it, others didn't. Money was of no interest to them because it didn't motivate them. Back then I struggled with that, but now I know how different we can all be.

Now when I look back, if I had used the sales DNA assessment,[6] I would have worked out that some of those people were more intrinsically motivated—they liked being part of a team and being part of greater success. Unfortunately, some of them were probably a little bit altruistic and shouldn't have been in sales. You know, they would put the customer before your company. They won't ask difficult questions; they want to be liked.

The big question is, have you ever wondered why your salespeople don't chase targets that hard? This is a giant trap, particularly if you want a scale.

And if they're happy doing reactive activities, not the hard yards that you need them to do, then finding the right remuneration balance is a fine line, depending on your business, strategy and growth plans.

So, it's important to understand how your salespeople are motivated before you generate compensation options to motivate sales.

Base Salary vs. On-Target Earnings (OTE)

The core element of sales compensation is base salary—the guaranteed earnings. It's what they're going to bring in on a monthly basis. It provides financial stability and baseline motivation. It should pay the bills; it should enable them to live comfortably.

In Australia in 2025, you've got compulsory superannuation (12%), and we also include fully maintained company vehicles to do the job in our packages (approximate annual value $20,000).

Then you tack on incentives like performance-based bonuses or commissions that drive focus, behaviour and growth. The way we want it to be.

When we're talking about a base, super and fully maintained company vehicle (FMCV), that's the fixed cost of employing a salesperson. On-target earnings (OTE) are the total fixed cost plus the incentive. This is the earnings if performance goals are met.

Now, with the base, be careful not to get caught with a high fixed cost and average results. When markets soften, this will seriously impact your bottom line.

This is why you see companies now going through processes of cost cutting. They will look at middle management or high-level management because they know they are a high fixed cost. You still need to be able to provide a return on investment at any level.

The split:

- For me personally, I like to work on a 60% base/40% incentive formula, or a 70/30.

The incentive should motivate your sales team to sell more and be rewarded for growth.

If you pay a higher base, they can get comfortable, and then the only person wanting to grow is you. That's not a good space to be in. I've been there before, and seen most of our clients face the same issue.

When we're hiring, we're looking at on-target earnings. What you offer should be a total package based on performance.

Extrinsic vs. Intrinsic motivation

Here is a story we quite often hear.

A leader calls, they want to get sales going, and I say, "Talk to me about your compensation program."

There's no incentive program. That's a problem. You need to have some sort of incentive program for a sales team.

It doesn't have to be all money. It can be other areas. As a leader, it is critical to understand what motivates each member of your sales team. The top 5% of sales performers—the elite salespeople—are typically more extrinsically motivated. It could also be a mix of extrinsic and intrinsic, which is fine.

This is why we use the sales DNA assessment—to find out how people are motivated. For example:

- Some people might like extra time off, like a four-day week.
- Some people might like other work perks.

Top performers want the rewards. They will shorten sales cycles because they'll push. They're ideal for a BDM or a leadership role.

About 50% of salespeople are intrinsically motivated, driven by purpose, mastery, and self-manufacture, and they're more suited for account management roles. You could look for a mixture of intrinsic and extrinsic incentives for a hybrid role.

Altruistic salespeople are typically in the bottom 10% of salespeople. They prioritise the customer over your company. They usually shift to more technical or product-based roles (or out of sales), so watch out for this pattern on CVs. It's a sign to be very cautious. Difficult conversations won't happen.

If you see people that have gone from an operations role into sales, then next thing you see, they've moved into product or they've moved into a technical sort of role. This is another sign to watch out for.

If you're looking for a BDM, these people won't be able to do it.

You can also look at how frequently they move on as well in sales positions, because it could be the fact that they're not performing and they're moving on, or they've been let go.

High-Performer New Hires

For high-performer new hires, you're potentially paying more to lure them from their current employer. They're not going to move for nothing. And let's face it. Top performers typically aren't even looking. If you've advertised, they won't have seen it.

COMPENSATION AND INCENTIVES

It's not all about the money. Most of us are motivated in different ways. Some are after flexibility, like working from home. It could be a hybrid role. It could be a combination of things they're looking for.

If you're looking to attract and bring top sales performers into your business, you really need to understand exactly what they're looking for to get them over.

For example, if your perfect candidate is asking for $130,000 base when you're offering $110,000, the current stats show that a salesperson who's been approached is trying to increase their current package by 10 to 30%.

But if it's a lateral move for somebody, (i.e., the same industry to another company), then you may get someone who's happy to move for 10 to 15% more. Or maybe they just want out and you might get lucky. But a sales performer who has a strong background and niche expertise could be looking for up to 30% more.

And if you're looking for a 30% increase in responsibility, for example, someone who's going to take on a sales management role or even a particular location that can vary between Brisbane, Sydney and Melbourne, then you may need to offer more. The potential problem with that is they could go back and renegotiate with their current employer. We do see that. It's part of the game.

We ask upfront when we're talking to someone: what compensation are you looking at? I've got a good memory.

But we also record a lot of our interviews to share with our clients, and the story can change sometimes when a candidate is asked again.

The benefits of having a partner like us who can help you understand more about the shifting current dynamics in remuneration, bonuses and options will ensure that you don't overpay for a salesperson who's not that good.

It's important to get back to why this person could be interested. Ask them the driving force behind them potentially moving to your business as it could give you more leverage.

They could be looking for flexibility or to get away from a poor manager, but remember, they could simply take the next best offer if they are actively looking for a job.

Quite often, a client will call us for advice on what to do. It's part of our service and long-term partnership for growth.

If you're caught in a spot and you're not sure, talk to us. We can look at where you're at, where you want to get to, and if needed, we can do a quick sales DNA assessment to make sure you're getting the right person who can sell!

It's easy to get caught in the heat of the moment, and let's face it, salespeople have had a lot of practice at interviewing. They've also had a lot of practice at negotiating, so they're going to go hard. They will say the right things when needed, and it's easy to say, "Yes, I'm going to come in and hunt for new business," but then when they get there, maybe they won't. Maybe they're not motivated to.

Existing Team

It is very easy to get out of whack with your compensation for your existing team, particularly if a salesperson's been there for many years and they've had CPI increases. All of a sudden, you might have an average salesperson on good money.

For example, if one of your salespeople is approached by a competitor, what are they worth from your perspective? What if they have been offered a $120-k base and you're paying them $100 k?

If you think they're worth $120 k, would you hire them again if they left? If you would, then ask them why they are worth $120 k, and hear them out. Be in the moment, be a good listener.

Ask them what they have done for you to ask for more. Or what else they will do to provide you with a return on your increased investment. They may be making up that they've been offered more.

I remember years ago when I asked for more money because I did physically need it, but I was aware of the current market and I knew that I wanted to buy my first home, I wanted to buy a new car, I wanted to get married, and I wanted to have a family. And I was performing to justify my request.

You need to uncover what's the driving force behind the reason a salesperson is asking for more money. Ask questions to find out what's in it for you if you do pay them more money:

- Is there more responsibility that you'll take on?
- Will you bring new business?
- What are you going to do to provide me with value?

It's a team effort and at the end of the day, you don't want to be rewarding someone who just has all your good customers. Pull the covers back:

- Are they your best sales performer or do they just have your good customers?

A performance-first approach is best to start with.

Sometimes you let someone leave, the next person comes along, you're having to pay them more and they're a worse performer than the one you had. But remember, when we recruit for our clients, we only hire from the top 20% that are identified and backed up with sales-specific, predictive data. We don't hire on gut feel.

Your existing salespeople will likely push the boundaries for more if they're an A-player. They will know they're a superstar and that you don't want to lose them.

But again, you still want to make sure you're able to get a return on your extra investment by making money from this salesperson. You don't want to lose a superstar, but it could be your chance to make a call on an average performer when one of your team asks for an increase.

My old boss, Peter Hyne, often said, "Jase, I need to sleep on that one. I need to have a think about it. Time out..."

For each salesperson, list their current base salary, assess whether it is too low, too high, or if you're not sure, and indicate whether they are a performer. This exercise will help you evaluate compensation alignment and identify opportunities for incentive adjustments.

This could be one of those moments to reflect. Just remember to be fair. Don't just look at sales results. Look at each salesperson's KPIs, are they meeting them all?

Look deeper into what new business these people have bought in and what has grown with existing business outside of your normal business relationships:

- What did they create?
- What did they progress?
- What new business did they close?
- And how much more can they do?

Base Salary Guides for Sales Leaders

You can download the white paper that includes base salary guides for leaders via the following QR code or visit www. jasonhowes.com.au/books/downloads.

The base salary guides for sales leaders are listed by years of relevant experience, with low, medium, high and median numbers as well, because there are geographical regions around Australia that don't sustain or don't require such a high salary level. For example, if you're in Sydney, you might be at a higher tier than if you're in regional Victoria or somewhere else where you may be able to get away with paying a low to medium-level salary.

Business Development Manager

A low salary for a BDM would be a $95 k base, median $110 k and higher level $130 k.

Now, again, by using a sales DNA assessment, we can assess someone's ability level. When we're recruiting, we aim to get someone in the 80 plus sales percentile.

If we evaluate somebody and they are under 50, you've got a problem. And if you're paying them a higher level, you've got even more of a problem.

Sales Manager

A sales manager may have 10+ years of experience and be managing around five people. A median base salary would be $150 k.

If it is a national sales manager role with someone who has 15 years' experience, then depending on the location, size of the team, the size of the company and the difficulty of the role, you could be talking a low base of $150 k, median $175 k and high $200 k.

You might also consider an option for a lower base for someone who backs themselves and is comfortable to have a crack at the title. You can lower the base and have uncapped incentives. But again, just remember you don't want to lose them if a competitor offers a higher base, and if they're not achieving incentives, they could jump. I've seen it happen many times.

Developing Effective Compensation Plans

Recent research shows that 44% of salespeople aren't motivated by their compensation plans.[7] But that isn't always the sales manager's fault. A lot of the time, no one's been taught how to build an effective compensation and incentive plan. It's quite difficult and market dynamics can change so quickly.

If you don't have an incentive plan to drive or motivate new business development, reach out anytime we'd love to help. It's a game-changer.

Maybe you have one, but it's old or never worked. Maybe it's time to drill down into it more. We've worked with clients who consistently push new boundaries to drive more new sales.

I prefer an incentive plan to pull the triggers that are important for your business right now. One that is aligned with your strategy. Whether that's winning new clients, growing market share or launching new products (which typically have a high failure rate, as high as 95%).[8] You'll need a good mix of base salaries and incentives to motivate your team to get the results you want.

The old saying goes, "Pay enough base so they can pay their bills and live, to keep your competitors away, but reward them generously for new business so they're hungry and chase the target and they don't sit back in reactive mode."

We have already spoken about the difference in motivation of a salesperson who has a home loan or wants nicer things like a better house, a holiday home and a better car, compared to one who owns everything and wants a good work/life balance.

COMPENSATION AND INCENTIVES

Your incentives should drive growth. Reward the behaviours that build your pipeline, that close new business opportunities, that retain valuable accounts or reactivate dormant valuable accounts.

If your incentive plan is too complex or too soft, it becomes a cost and not a catalyst for growth. I think paying incentives quarterly is the best way. Sometimes you can work with monthly targets to drive continuous motivation, but use no more than two to four variables in your incentive plan. Keep it simple, keep it visible, and keep it tied to outcomes.

Consider creating leading indicators for earning a bonus. For example, a salesperson managing their territory plan effectively, getting their reports in on time, getting proposals done in on time, complying with CRM reporting and activities could earn a $500 bonus per quarter. That incentive will get them doing the activities you need them to do. If you get everyone on your team doing it, then you'll see results and consistency.

You could also look at performance multipliers, especially if your market slows down. You could use 1.25X or a 1.5X incentive accelerator for exceeding target in a super-competitive market.

There are always ways to use incentives to leverage where you're at. Try new things. If you're sitting here now and you're not paying incentives, your salespeople could have looked at the end of the financial year and given up because they're behind target. You need to look at ways to get things going again.

The other area you look at is a SPIF (sales performance incentive fund)—a short-term incentive for a key product launch or seasonal pushes. We've seen this done effectively as well. It can sometimes get opportunities that are stuck in a pipeline moving again. It can get salespeople selling with more urgency because they've got to get the sale closed this quarter to get their incentive.

I've seen this work before. It'll also show you straight away the ones that are willing to have a crack. And then you can look at the ones who are not having a crack. Are they in the right role? Potentially not.

You can reward people for activating a new account or reactivating a dormant account in a slow market. They could earn a $250 flat fee for doing that, or whatever you think is realistic for your business to reflect the importance of doing this. But again, be careful, make sure they haven't reactivated an account just because your competitor is out of stock. I like to put a clause in that says the account must be buying on an ongoing basis or in a regular pattern.

A non-financial incentive is time in lieu. Some people could be happier to take a half a day off or a full day a month in lieu of being paid compensation. Time off could be more valuable than money to them.

When I was a leader, I loved going out in the field with our salespeople. In the car, on a trip and in the moment. We should know as a leader where each salesperson is at and what motivates them:

- What's happening in their life?
- What's happening with their family?
- What's their personal goals? Are they aligned with yours?
- Where are they looking to get to?

Because if you don't ask those questions and they're a good performer, someone else will. If you're not out there spending time in the field with your salespeople, or not having that good 1:1 time, then it's an opportunity for a problem to develop.

Best Practices for Incentive Programs to Work

- They must align with your business goals and your strategy.
- Know your costs. How much can you afford to pay?
- Know the ROI you need to achieve.
- Know your competition. How competitive is your incentive program in the market? What's working for other companies? Why is it working and how can you leverage off those opportunities?
- Make your incentives achievable and motivating, not unrealistic.

- Have clarity. Make your incentives easy for your salespeople to calculate. For example, if they do secure a large order or a large customer, they should be able to calculate very quickly how much they will earn.
- Develop leading KPIs that are aligned with your incentives to help you speed up the closing of sales.
- Reward the winning of new business rather than just servicing existing business (for example, by paying a higher percentage incentive for the first 12 months).
- Reward in-house team members for booking meetings with dream clients for your BDM or account managers that lead to business. Spread the love around.
- Be agile. Things can change.

Be Careful with Commission Incentives

I'll share when I was on the road back in good old 1999, pre-GST. For those that were in sales, a huge number of sales were pulled forward to the first half of the year to avoid the 10% GST coming in that year on July 1. Little did we know that we probably paid more as prices increased. Demand was at crazy levels, then it all dropped on July 1.

I'd just purchased my first home. It's a big step as you know. I was doing a lot of renovations to it, and they were solely funded by my commission. At that point, we were actually paid 0.2% commission on all sales, but with the boom of the looming GST, my sales went from $1.2 million up to about $2 million per month. It helped, but it was rewarding to see the hard work pay off for increasing market share and getting a piece of the action. You could sell anything, if you couldn't then....

Suddenly, I was earning four grand commission per month. Back then, that was a lot of money. $4,000 in 1999 is equivalent today to $7,627 per month. Didn't the handbrake come on very hard after GST, I remember my sales dropped back to a million dollars a month, so I wasn't getting as much commission. I'd just organised to get a new driveway, and it hit me hard.

But the commission drove me to sell more to hit quota. I've always been motivated personally by success, the love of what I do and contributing to the team, but also, a love of the $.

However, the trap was that if orders weren't supplied, which was quite often back then, we did miss out on a lot of money. Considerable amounts, but that's manufacturing and not uncommon.

If you're a leader, you need to be cautious that if your salespeople are getting the orders and you're not getting those orders out from an operations perspective, that can be a real problem. I've seen salespeople leave companies because of that.

If your company has no margin restrictions, that can be a concern as well with commission incentives. Because if salespeople sell products at a low margin, then they still make the same commission.

Things can change with or without the influence of a salesperson or your business (like the COVID period), so you need to be aware of that with the structure of your incentives. Include an appendix to your incentive program that deals with changing conditions. Then if or when something changes, you won't need to update the entire employment contract and have it re-signed.

We can help you with appendices or any other area of your incentive program.

Look After Your Top Performers

Recent research shows that 70% of salespeople miss budget.[9] So make sure you look after your top performers. Incentive options for them may include a percentage of gross profit, like a split incentive of 50% sales and 50% gross profit. Or a straight commission might work best.

Your incentives must motivate your salespeople to hunt. The big questions: should they be on the bus? Are they in the right role?

COMPENSATION AND INCENTIVES

The last thing you want, and we see it regularly, is to lose top performers and get stuck with your underperformers looking after your best accounts.

If you're in a market downturn and most of your growth will come from your competitors, then your salespeople need to be able to create value and close new opportunities, not just sit back like I've seen over the years.

Some salespeople are just waiting and praying for a market shortage. They've never really been taught how to create and win new business opportunities. This is typically where account managers struggle. A lot of them have never been trained.

There are no systems, there's no processes, and they struggle to get to decision-makers. They're talking to the wrong people, and they're not confident or motivated enough to make the move.

I've heard salespeople like that say, "I'll just keep calling on them. Something will happen one day, they'll come over to me."

If you really want to take the gloves off and get the best people into your business, then offer an uncapped incentive program. But make sure you're right on target with what you're going to do because it's easy for an uncapped program to get out of control. I've seen it go pear-shaped.

Another thing we've seen is that some sales leaders would rather reward the entire business or team with a percentage of profit. However, each salesperson needs to hit quota to qualify. I'm not completely sold on that one. I've seen it fail and it can cause animosity if one department fails without any control from others. I don't like taking the responsibility off individuals.

Setting up a leaderboard can also be effective. Put the score up. One of our clients did it, and it immediately impacted their team. They could see where they were at, and what they needed to do to reach their targets. And they were rewarded, even with simple things like a free coffee or lunch (food works incredibly well).

Most CRMs have built-in dashboards with incredible stats to focus on. Do you have access to "live sales data"?

I think it's good to show where everyone's at—who's achieving and who's not, to put a little bit of healthy competition there.

No CRM, No Scoreboard
No Leading KPIs, No Coaching

2025 AFL Qualifying Final		
COLLINGWOOD	11.13	(79)
ADELAIDE	8.7	(55)

Performance Metrics	Current	Target
Sales Cycle days	48	37
Win Rate	25%	38
Avg Deal Size	$14,000	$19,000
Pipeline Value	$250,000	$295,000

Leading KPIs	Current	Target
Prospect Created	3	5
Qualified Prospects	2	3
Site Calls Completed	4	7

Sales isn't guesswork — it's game strategy.
Your CRM is the scoreboard

Summary

- Sales compensation is one of the most powerful and often overlooked drivers of sustainable business growth.
- As markets shift and buyer behaviour evolves, leaders must think about and rethink how they pay, motivate and retain sales talent.
- When done well, compensation doesn't just drive revenue. It inspires performance, creates loyalty and embeds a strong sales culture.
- The white paper introduces a practical and proven model designed to evaluate and optimise sales compensation strategies. Our guide also includes a snapshot of our recommended compensation

benchmarks for sales leaders, hunters and managers across B-to-B sectors in Australia in 2025, and includes actionable tools to build incentive schemes to reward and motivate your team.

You can download more information on online by visiting: www.jasonhowes.com.au/books/downloads.

CHAPTER 5

Attracting Top Sales Talent

Companies used to hold more power. If someone wasn't performing, they'd simply replace them. There were more options.

But strong performers can hold a lot of power these days, and some leaders don't like it.

Recruitment cycles can move very quickly. Right now, with large numbers of redundancies, more candidates are flooding the market.

And there are less jobs, with hiring freezes. Many hiring managers are like, "Cool, more to pick from," but here's a few major hurdles we're hearing. You also must seriously consider the chance that you may hire someone else's underperformer who can start straight away ...

Top performers are shooting from the hip. If they're not happy with a company, if they're not happy with leadership, if they're not happy with culture or where they're at, then they will move on quite quickly and there's no turning back. See you later! I've seen it many times, even with some stars we're recruited. It's disappointing for our clients and us. Sometimes you don't know what you've got until it's gone.

Supply and demand are tightening. Population growth has slowed. Companies wanting to grow sales are caught short.

There are more baby boomers, they're cashed up, and thinking about retirement. Many are not interested in the hard yards anymore.

Plenty from Gen X, my generation, are cashed up from property, and they're also not that keen on taking on key roles like business development because it's a tough grind. I get it. They're more comfortable in leadership or account management positions.

It's very difficult to go from leadership back to field sales. Maybe it's my age bracket, or that we're searching for high level business development, sales hunters and leaders with experience, but many are looking for less stress, with less commitment.

We're competing for talent.

Candidates look on Seek, LinkedIn, Glassdoor for reviews on your business. Or they're following you on social platforms. It's important to check your online position.

I want you to stop right here to go and do that.

If you Google your company, if you look under reviews, look at scores, where are you at? From your perspective, how do you look online?

Quick Talent Attraction Tip: Get your team to go into some of these platforms and leave messages of their experience and how they love working for you. It will help you attract talent. In interviews, candidates are potentially interviewing you just as much. That's not a bad sign—you want a fit and an alignment. Both parties should be excited to work together for the good things to come.

That's why a lot of clients we work with prefer to utilise our team to help recruit. Even though some want to save money, you don't have time. However, others may choose to do it themselves and we will support you to save money, if that is your priority.

If you're looking to attract talent, remember that you're going to work with this person every day. It still amazes me why a lot of companies don't invest more time and money into recruitment.

Maybe they've given up finding someone strong, and a lot of companies are now settling for average performers. A lot of companies are settling for average performance because they don't think they can find anyone better.

The best sales talent isn't looking. They're in a job. The big question is "How can you attract them to your company if they're not looking?"

Let's just pause there for a sec.

Many hiring managers (most who have never been trained) unfortunately take the quick and easy road. Many are time-poor; not wanting to invest in the process. I've been there. Leadership often doesn't want to pay for recruiters because they've had bad experiences. I know, I did too.

Typically, your priority is to find someone with industry experience, preferably that's worked at a major competitor, or who knows your clients. I speak from experience here in hiring a lot of salespeople. Just because someone came from a major competitor or the industry, it doesn't guarantee that they will succeed at your company.

Every business is different. Most roles are different. Different market share, different dynamics, different strengths and weaknesses.

I've seen it quite often where an apparent top salesperson at another company had all the good customers. I've said that many times. Pull back the covers:

- What did they generate and win themselves?
- Ask for success stories. Bring this up with your reference checking!

This chapter will provide you with more ways to attract talent to make sure you're hiring a sales professional from the top 20%, not the bottom 50% where a lot of salespeople fall.

Here are some key areas that you can focus on to attract top talent.

Top Sales Talent Want to Work with Companies that Make a Difference

We're seeing more of this. They want to work for companies that:

- Add global value.
- Have a culture they're proud of.
- Have goals beyond making money.
- Care about the environment.
- Share profits for meaningful causes.
- Offer amazing products and services.
- Lead with innovation by constantly creating new products and services.
- Allow them to lead a product or brand.
- Are exciting to work at.
- Encourage salespeople to take risks, share ideas and find new opportunities.

Top Sales Talent Want to Use Tools to Help Them Succeed

Check point:
- What is your website like?
- What is our social media presence and following?
- Do you have a marketing team that will support your vision?

These are all important milestones to attract top talent. They want and need all the tools to succeed.

They want to work somewhere that they can thrive, where they have shared beliefs, for a company that is fair, that communicates well, that offers professional development, and that invests and genuinely cares for their people. They want a company that has strong leadership where people want to work for your leadership team.

They're confident about their ability. They know that good leaders not only help companies succeed, but they also keep salespeople engaged and motivated, and they have joint goals. They're driven to succeed.

There are effective managers who respect their salespeople and recognise their family and their positive contributions to work.

Top Sales Talent Want to Have Access to Leadership

They want to be able to talk with CEOs and department managers. They want to be able to have a career trajectory. They want opportunities for growth. We hear a lot of salespeople say they are leaving a company where they see no future growth for them.

When we work with our clients, we've been building sales trajectories from internal sales to account management, from account management to BDM, from BDM to sales management to sales leadership.

This is the sort of thing that the younger generation is looking for. But they need to earn their stripes and sometimes can get impatient. They need your support to succeed. Work/life balance is very important to them.

Top Sales Talent Want Attractive Compensation Packages and Perks

No secrets there. It not only attracts talented salespeople, but it also helps retain them. You need to find out what motivates them, both financially and non-financially. It's only a part of the recipe, but companies are trying many ways to attract top talent by offering additional benefits. For example, health insurance, profit share, share options or wellness programs. Here is a list of others that we've come across, and maybe some could easily be implemented into your compensation package?

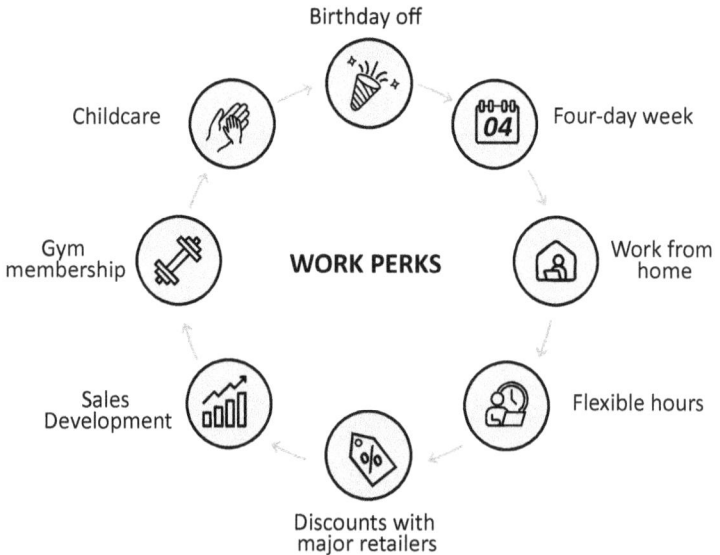

Birthday off

Childcare

Four-day week

Gym membership

WORK PERKS

Work from home

Sales Development

Flexible hours

Discounts with major retailers

I'll share a success story—Knotwood, one of our largest clients. We're proud of our business partnership. They just celebrated their 16th birthday and brought their whole team together on the Gold Coast to celebrate it. Their culture is amazing—they have strong leaders who are passionate about what they do.

They lead from the front, they have a great culture, they're always innovating new products, they support Australian companies and industries and the environment. When we're recruiting for Knotwood, it makes our job better because we have the confidence to be able to place top candidates. We have the confidence to be able to attract more top people into the role.

And our relationship is very strong because they're very busy doing what they do well and they lean on us for sales training and development, and they lean on us to help build a high-performance sales team by hiring and attracting A-players.

"We want to make a solution-focused and solution-first system. But we want our people to be empowered, backed and trusted, and to trust us to deliver on this. So, it is not a business of micromanagement or anything like that. It's very much, we want to empower and trust our people and grow them. We do a lot of internal promotion and internal development as well.

We have a team of 30 in internal and external sales. I want to ensure that it's a high-performance, empowered team that's trusted and trusts us, can assist us on our growth journey, and we can make sure we can assist and grow the people that we have.

So, we're doing more sales in New Zealand. We export to Hawaii. We're setting up new manufacturing in the US in Phoenix, Arizona. And we have a team in the UK as well.

We're on a very good solid growth trajectory. It's a very exciting, amazing place to work.

I wear my heart on my sleeve and I'm very passionate about what I do, but working with a team like this makes my day just to see it, especially when our values are very aligned."

—Brendan O'Shea, National Sales Manager, Knotwood Australia and New Zealand

Taking the Guesswork Out of Hiring Top Sales Talent

I remember when I was a sales leader, someone said. "You always need to be hiring from a leader's perspective."

You need to invest in attending industry events, conferences, or wherever your tribe hangs out. You meet people, you see how they act, you see how they teach, or how they talk to prospects. It gives you an opportunity to build a relationship with a lot of other people within your industry.

And that is how I made a lot of successful hires. I also made some unsuccessful hires.

As I've consistently said, you want to be attracting the right type of talent, not just salespeople with industry experience. You need ones that can sell!

I used to make a big effort to get to know others. I'd be in the moment, asking them questions. But don't just rely on getting along well with someone.

That's why we use a sales DNA assessment tool[10] to provide more confidence about a person's sales ability, tactics and mindset.

It removes the bias, and it shows us exactly where they sit in comparison to everyone else. Before you even consider investing your valuable time into interviewing someone, you can use the tool to see where they're at.

You will be shocked! Some people don't take sales seriously; it's just a job. In sales, you need passion, grit and commitment to do whatever it takes to succeed, as long as it's ethical.

The tool we use is predictive and provides sales-specific data. There's no guesswork, no going by gut feel, and you'll make less hiring errors. And less hiring errors will save you a lot of money.

Many industries have not invested in the professional development of their leaders, and this flows down the line and affects the quality of salespeople. A performance gap appears, which can lead to customer churn, missed opportunities and the inability to reach targets. Unfortunately, a leader will only lead like they've been taught, and the performance gap can be huge!

I was fortunate to have some good mentors, but I still invested in my own professional development in sales, managing national accounts, marketing and leadership.

That's why most tend to hire from within an industry, because they know someone, or someone that knows that person. I've seen it happen many times.

The other option is to hire from the younger generation, looking for a positive attitude. I tend to like people who have played sports, who have a competitive nature, who are motivated, and who you can train into a future role.

By having a strong network, and writing a job ad that attracts top performers, we can make a big impact with your search.

We also leverage a lot of our talent acquisition by using AI sourcing tools for our outreach program. We invest heavily in tech to provide our recruitment team with the best tools.

We search geographical regions by specific segments, like building materials, construction, manufacturing, hire and rental as examples.

We can then drill down to years of experience and average tenure, and add a Boolean search for specific products or key areas that are most critical for you. On one search, we came up with 5,000 potential candidates.

This is on top of us advertising on Seek, Indeed, LinkedIn and all our social platforms.

They won't all be a good fit, but tech and automation allow us to filter quickly, access contact details and send outreach targeted campaigns. We utilise multiple platforms to identify and then attract top candidates. The main difference is that we're consistently recruiting, not like hiring managers who are typically caught out and need to fill the position quickly.

Traditionally, most Australian companies would only put an ad on Seek and then hope and pray they get someone to apply. If we did that, then we wouldn't be any better than anyone else offering recruitment services. It is only a part of our process (and in the future your process if you want to attract top talent). I would rather get the best salesperson from a wider pool than just relying on a job ad.

Because of our large network, we often get 200+ applications. The number will vary based on the location, job title, company, what remuneration is offered, and the market dynamics. Recruitment is a fast-moving segment.

We save a lot of time with our automation; we do get a lot of people that apply without reading the ad. There's a lot of time-wasters. There's a lot of people who apply for jobs to tick a box so that they can receive Centrelink/government services. It's an absolute pain.

They say that it can take up to 20 hours of your time to go through applications. Many of our clients who were previously hiring in-house got to the end with no one suitable to hire. They were too busy, the talent pool wasn't great or they were undecided. I've been their numerous times as a sales leader in the past.

You should be starting to realise that we're different from traditional recruiters. Unfortunately, I've had experience with recruiters basically throwing anyone at me with industry experience. Hit and hope!

My priority back then was to hire the best candidate. Whether they were from our ad, if I approached someone or even if a recruiter floated one to me. Unfortunately, the company that I was at, like many, banned using recruiters after a bad experience, so I had to rely on our internal process for many years alone, and then our HR person was part-time and really didn't help. It was left to me.

And I understand that in a lot of cases it's like a round robin with many recruiters. They'll place a candidate who doesn't work out, they'll then replace that person. They get desperate. They just want to get you off their back.

You're like a monkey hanging on. Trying to get value for your large investment, I get it.

That's not how we operate. We build an avatar for the perfect type of talent for your business. What attributes, skills and mindset are the top of your list? This will vary for a particular role.

When we're working with our clients, we build specific criteria for each role integrated into a sales DNA assessment. We have account management criteria. We have BDM criteria. We have sales management criteria. But what traits are you looking for? We build these in.

It could be that they must be competitive. You might want someone resilient because you're going to get a lot of rejections. Someone with a strong work ethic. Someone with past success in winning new business.

That is our most common role, a sales hunter! An experienced, extrinsically motivated A-player for a business development role. Someone who's motivated to achieve targets and get rewarded for their hard work. They thrive on the thrill of the chase.

It could be industry-specific, like building materials or manufacturing.

We try not to get too tied up in, for example, steel or hardware experience. Instead, we will look for building materials or construction industry to open the talent pool up. It gives us more choice.

We will always search for what our client wants first, then move to the next level if the right person isn't found.

We like to look for people who have invested in their professional development or done sales training. But we still do the assessment as not all sales training is effective, and not everyone buys into it.

We also consider whether they have worked at any companies that are good breeding grounds.

Fortunately for us when doing the sales DNA assessment, which is our first step in the process after someone's applied, we can see their results. We can see their confidence in how they've answered. And whether they meet your specific criteria for the role. This is the crystal ball at work. Think of it like you've fired an arrow, it's mid-air but you need to ensure the trajectory is at the right loft, heading towards your target.

Next, it's easier to drill into the "recommended" candidates resume and see if their experience is what you're looking for, and that they're not job hopping every 1–2 years. You want more longevity to make your ROI.

If you don't use an assessment, it's like driving down the road at night with your lights off and you've got a hairpin corner coming. If you don't know where you're going, you're in trouble.

Having the assessment is like having a crystal ball. It's like having your lights on. You can see where you're going before you hire someone.

I'll share a quick sales story here.

One of our best recruits years ago was from the telco industry, plodders won't survive. It's competitive, they're motivated to sell more, and they're rewarded well. They also have strong sales processes to follow.

So, we saw sales experience in business development, and a strong resume application.

For us, anyone with sales experience also goes through our screening, not just industry experience, in case we find a "diamond in the rough". And we did.

He had no relevant building materials industry experience, but when he entered the hardware industry, he absolutely nailed it. I always say to our clients, give me a top sales professional any day, rather than just industry experience!

The sales DNA assessment quickly uncovered his sales ability.

If someone pops up when you are hiring and could be a diamond in the rough, we can put them through the sales DNA assessment tool to remove any bias and ensure you're making the right decision.

This guy negotiated hard on the way in. He knew he was worth more money and our client needed a real good hunter. He was a go-getter.

One thing I loved about this gentleman, Dave, I'll call him, is that he's very good at building relationships quickly. Early in the sales process, he really built a good rapport, and he also sold very consultatively. He had looked closely and listened closely to the challenges of the industries.

And then once he worked out what worked, he then scaled what he did and followed good sales processes. He had a really good way to get new opportunities across the line. He would ask for the order, not just once or twice, but until he got it.

Now, like most top sales professionals, this guy had a home loan. He wanted to earn more, so he pushed very hard.

His sales cycle was quite short. He knew how to ask the right questions, and he wouldn't take no for an answer.

And I loved that about Dave.

He was very persistent, but he also got to the decision-makers and asked the difficult questions. He got products on the shelf.

Potentially the "best salesperson" is right in front of you. Remember this one. Most of the top performers we've recruited are from outside the typical "product experience" category.

Building a Scorecard

We recommend building a scorecard.

We do this with our role criteria. Hopefully, in previous chapters you've started to think more closely on what's worked and what hasn't worked for you in the past. You've defined your role, and now you should be getting a clearer pathway to hire a team more aligned to your company's strategy.

You want to be able to see what your perfect salesperson looks like. You can then use this scorecard in your screening and interviewing process. It helps you to score accurately and consistently, and it will even help you to ask the right questions. When you work with us and putting people through the sales DNA assessments, it creates interview questions for you. It will pick the gaps, and even provide what typical candidate responses.

A lot of us aren't really that good at interviewing, so it's a big bonus. We were never taught how to ask the right questions at interviews.

Creating an Advert That Will Help You Attract Sales Talent

You need a compelling ad that makes candidates think, *"Wow, that's my job!"* We get that quite often from candidates. They'll say, "Hey, look, I read the job ad, and I thought, that's me."

Your job ad needs to provide an exciting vision. The standout points or the first sentence must catch the eye of top talent. Your ad's stats should demonstrate maximum impact, so check yours, and always aim for a higher result. One that we recently advertised, had 7.6x better applications than industry standard. Or 67% more views.

Quick Ad Tip: We see a lot of companies that put a full position description up. Minimise the 'About the company' information, and include more about what's in it for top talent.

We also include the OTE, and any perks in the ad itself.

When I look back to my own time as a sales leader pre-AI, I openly admit that if someone left, I would pull up the last job ad, change it slightly, and get it online as quickly as I could.

I didn't write a compelling job advert. I was never trained how to do it. I was time- poor, and I just rolled the dice.

A lot of people have done the same things over the years. How long has it been since you reviewed your job advert?

But times have changed now. Your ad needs to be short and sweet. It needs to be mobile- friendly. And to make a quick impact for someone to hit 'Apply'. The latest research shows that 64% of applicants are now reading job ads on a mobile phone.[11]

You should lead with confidence that your company is the place to work. A good idea is to record a professional video about the culture, the business, and why people should come and work at your company. Be proud of your business. We have a video we use when we're hiring, and quite often I have candidates say that they felt like we care more than other companies.

It's also impressive to see a message from the CEO or the owner and some of your team. One of our clients interviews with teammates, so once you've attracted top talent, let potential candidates hear what it's like to work with them and/or your leaders.

Here is a guide that you can use to develop your ad copy.

ATTRACTING TOP SALES TALENT

Writing The Ad Template

Sell the vision/dream _____

You must have prior success selling

_____
(enter your what)

to _____
(enter Decision Maker Title)

of _____
(enter target customer)

in a _____
(enter the biggest challange)

You have _____
(enter required skills)

Experience _____
with _____(enter parallel experiences)

_____ helpful but
not required.

Travel to _____ required. We need you to

earn more than _____ and our top producers

make _____ .

About the company and why us (location, benefits)

_____

Call to action _____

Steps of your _____
process

You can download this ad writing guide at www.jasonhowes.
com.au/books/downloads.

Quick Ad Tips:

- If you're just relying on paid job ads, then you're in trouble. Potentially, you will be hiring someone else's underperformer. You need a wider talent pool to select from.
- The job ad posting should be done across multiple platforms but remember, you're looking to attract top talent, and they're probably not even looking.

If you're struggling to attract more talent, talk with us about leveraging our large network and our AI-sourcing tool. We've always got jobs across Australia, so we could even have a quality candidate in our talent pool (or we'll know where to find them). We're always talking with candidates, every day.

If you have a long-term sales talent model, it's a good idea for us to find out more about what type of role you want to fill, then we can work away, confidentially, to search for you.

Just remember, a talented sales professional may not be looking today but could be next week, next month or next year. We play the long game, never the short game.

Now, here's a little bit of homework for you to finish off this chapter:

- What does your industry think of your company or say about it?
- Ask some of your best clients why they partner with you. This can help to attract top talent.

You want to hear the truth because if there are problems, top talent will run away. Problems like:

- There's been a lot of turnover.
- A questionable culture.
- Insufficient remuneration.
- A leader that people don't want to work for.

If you're facing these challenges, then unfortunately you may have to overpay to get someone because you don't have a strong reputation. You will likely have to pay a premium because top candidates will know that it may not last if they transition to your business.

When I used to go to conferences as a sales leader, people used to come and say things like:

- "Hey, I want to work with you."
- "I heard your company is good to work at. And you as a leader."
- "I like what you're doing."
- "I like the culture."

As I've said, top talent may not be looking right now, but things can change very quickly. Always be in hiring mode for top talent. I've had companies find a position for someone because they see their talent. They see the opportunities in them. They'll find a job for them.

We're doing that with a client now. We're bringing back top-level candidates, and this leader is strategically placing them to where their strengths are. He knows that he needs top quality talent.

There is a lot of restructuring going on right now. There's a lot of redundancies and people are getting a little bit nervous. So, there are opportunities there. You've also got a lot of new leadership appointments, and with new leadership, the first three months tends to see a lot of change.

It is a big job being a leader. Effective recruitment is a large part of a leader's job. Hiring salespeople, and building new relationships. There are a lot of boxes to tick, and it is a big investment in attracting top talent, but it will pay off.

With our help, you can streamline your hiring process, replicate it consistently, and when someone does leave, you're ready to replace them efficiently with a proven top performer.

CHAPTER 6

Removing Bias from Hiring

Most hiring managers aren't aware that their biases influence their hiring.

I'll share some critical roadblocks here that hold many of us back from hiring quality sales professionals, and we'll also use a little bit of science in this chapter. I've researched how bias affects hiring decisions and I've also seen it from my own experience in filling positions.

Bias starts with looking solely for candidates with industry or product experience instead of sales ability. Some leaders we speak with are not even willing to accept experience and sales ability in connected or similar industries.

However, leaders looking for new ways to hire have embraced our resources to recruit incredible sales professionals, not just order-takers.

Most of us are not even aware that bias plays a huge part when hiring. It can also affect who is potentially even shortlisted. It's not only employer bias, but it also can be candidate bias as well. Salespeople tend to like to work for similar companies.

You also want to make sure that your job descriptions use language to ensure that no bias comes into play from the outset.

Personally, my approach is simple: always hire the best person for the job. Male, female, earlier in their career or highly experienced —whatever aligns with your role priorities.

Types of Bias

Bias in hiring is often learned and shaped by many variables.

For some, it may be gender bias.

For others, it may be age bias, where a client assumes younger candidates cost less or are more motivated.

Resumes may not be shared because of an unconscious bias to one name over another. Perhaps, you had a bad experience with someone called Jeremy? Or Jerry! If so, that is your bias.

It could be a bias away from corporate experience towards a smaller family business.

Or a candidate may be selected over others because, as a mate of mine said, "I could see myself having a beer with this person." Again, that's a bias.

Research shows that 30% of interviewers or hiring managers make up their mind in the first five minutes if a candidate will move forward or not.[12]

Unconscious bias refers to judgements and assumptions that our brains make without even being conscious or aware of it happening.

Closely related to unconscious bias is **affinity bias** in which people tend to gravitate to others who act similar, who look similar, and do similar things that they do.

I personally like people that have a bit of a get up and go, people that are motivated, potentially people that have played some sport and been successful in training and competing.

And I didn't even realise that over the years, particularly if I was recruiting in Victoria, I'd always want to know what team candidates barracked for. It became a bit of a joke with my interviewees.

You do need to be careful, otherwise, you can end up having a team of people like yourself. I've seen this with energetic and motivated leaders. If I speak to their teams, they'll often all talk the same, even to the point of acting very similarly.

There are so many industries that have a history of relying on a particular individual and that could create a bias to hire people just like them. Or to be hiring people who they're comfortable with.

However, the most successful organisations are those that intentionally seek out motivated, results- orientated people who will challenge the status quo.

A lack of diversity in the workplace can impact the bottom line of companies. But diversity isn't just a checkbox. It's also a strategic advantage. This can have a ripple effect of building an exceptional team that extracts exceptional candidates.

While hiring only people with industry or product experience may seem like a logical choice, it very quickly narrows down the talent pool to a very small number. Typically, these people are also being pursued by other companies within your industry because they're looking for similar attributes. And they're getting paid more than they should be in my experience.

That strategy obviously limits the recruitment of new candidates with new perspectives. It also can lead to a revolving-door effect where salespeople continue to go from one company to the next because of their knowledge and experience in specific products.

We've been breaking this cycle for many years now and helping bring in fresh industry talent. And we've been successful in doing that. Most clients who were originally hesitant to take that approach now comment on how much better their new hires are by comparison. We get told that they are "next level", ramping up in half the time, and quickly picking up on product knowledge.

I remember we had one company who got annoyed because we were advertising that we do recruitment and were worried that we were going to take all the good candidates from our industry. I didn't have the heart to tell the guy, but unfortunately, there's a lot of people we won't hire from our industry, because many have never been trained or don't invest in their own professional development.

We work the other way around. We bring in top-level talent to our industry, the top 20%, to help both our industry and our clients. I stand proud and confident in saying this, and we back it up.

A high level of the people we're hiring share operational or commercial similarities. It could be manufacturing, wholesale, electrical, glass, plumbing or other related industries. The key is finding whose experience complements the role's objectives and their adaptability.

Some clients prefer their recruits having a degree. Many strong performers we've hired do have a degree or have owned their own business. It's part of the mix that leads to strong, experienced performers.

It can create or contribute to having a unique perspective to help foster better problem-solving, better innovation, and even more strategic planning.

Objective Assessment

We follow steps to ensure we remove bias, and we also push back a little bit against our clients if they are being held back by bias. The assessment tool does its work without any bias, and it's 95% accurate.[13]

If a candidate is recommended, they proceed to the next stage, where we dive deeper into their resumes, aligning their results versus their experience and their application.

We help our clients to shortlist as they go. We do a quick phone call with five to seven shortlisted candidates to confirm that:

- They are a good fit.
- They align with what you're looking for.
- The remuneration is acceptable.
- They've fully understood the job advertisement (which unfortunately, a lot of people don't).

At the end of the phone call, ask yourself these questions:

- How did they present themselves?
- Were they good on the phone?
- Were they a clear communicator?
- Did they ask questions?

At this point, we still haven't seen this person we're recruiting for you. There's no bias. You don't know what they look like or how they dress.

If they're keen to discuss the job in more detail and if we think they could be a good choice for our position, we will then schedule a 15-minute video interview with three to five candidates. From a time perspective for the hiring manager, this is not a significant investment (45–75 minutes).

Although we can get 200+ applications per job because we source from a wide pool, the assessment tool efficiently narrows it down to a very fine shortlist of sales professionals who could do the job, based on sales-specific, predictable data, not gut feel.

The next key area of our process is a structured interview agenda with predefined questions so that we can make sure that we can have an accurate scorecard on our opinion from interviewing each person. Once again, this helps to remove bias.

We ask the same questions to every candidate, in the same order. Our questions are crafted from either the ones recommended through the sales DNA assessment and/or the ones we have generated for a specific role.

What can happen if you don't have a structured list of questions is that you may like somebody and click with them, then avoid asking some of the hard questions that you may ask someone else. If you do, that's your bias coming in. You want to give everybody the same opportunity to tell their story and to showcase if they're fit for the role.

The questions we craft focus on asking about the candidates themselves, including why they applied for the job and what they're looking for. We don't really talk much in this interview. We try to keep it quite informal. We want to understand more about each candidate, including how quickly they can build rapport, how they communicate and how they sell.

Key Takeaways

- Make sure you write inclusive job advertisements so that a diverse range of candidates can enter your recruitment pool. Don't make it solely about industry experience.
- Standardise your interview process to make sure every candidate has the same opportunities.
- The sales DNA assessment tool we use is job-specific and unbiased. It doesn't know who each candidate is, where they live or which gender they are. It only evaluates each candidate's fit with the client and their criteria to determine their likelihood of succeeding a specific role.

  Your team can use this tool to learn how to recruit like an expert, and gain access to all the training and documentation to remove bias and make sound hiring decisions.
- If you can remove bias from your hiring process, then you will uncover opportunities to hire top-performing sales professionals.

CHAPTER 7

How to Select the Best Talent

Let's briefly recap what we've covered so far:

- You've looked at your current team's abilities to execute your strategy (Chapter 1).
- We've had a look to ensure that you're making an ROI on your new hires and existing sales team (Chapter 2).
- You've drilled into role definition to ensure you're clear on what's required to succeed (Chapter 3).
- We've dived deep into what compensation looks like to support your growth and to drive new business opportunities and maximise your ROI (Chapter 4).
- We've looked at creative strategies for talent acquisition to see how you can bring the best candidates to the table instead of advertising a role and getting very little response (Chapter 5).

- We've talked about how to remove bias from your hiring decisions by using the sales DNA assessment tool[14] and associated processes right from the start of your hiring journey (Chapter 6).

We are now at the most important topic—selecting the best sales talent.

If you don't use an efficient hiring tool, and you get a large volume of applications, then it takes a huge amount of work to sift through them, shortlist, screen, interview, reference check, etc. It can take up to 20 hours per hire when you're already juggling multiple balls and trying to hit sales budgets.

You could be reading this thinking, *"We're only getting under 50 applications."* That's not necessarily a good thing. The previous chapters covered key areas that will help you attract more candidates to widen your potential talent pool, which is crucial. Try revisiting these chapters. Potentially your job advert was very specific on what is required to succeed in this role, and it scared away candidates who weren't willing to take on the responsibility. It could be for a combination of reasons.

Sometimes the best salespeople are right in front of you, or the best ones that tick some boxes but not all. How do you know without having a crystal ball?

We can use our process to get you the best salespeople on your team. If you remove one important step, then it could impact your outcome. It's a big decision at $200 k per annum. Over 5 years, it's equivalent to purchasing a new home.

Recruiting for the first time is intense. Think of the new hiring manager, or one that's been doing it for a while now without any training or process. Scary isn't it? A high percentage of new hiring managers take it on themselves because they feel a need to prove their ability. I get that point of view from being in the same position myself, but it's a very risky game to play, and I've seen poor recruitment cost the hiring manager their own job if their hires fail. Leadership needs to step in, like one of our clients did to stop the damage to their company brand.

Automation and technology will save you time so that if someone pops up in your network looking for a job, you've now got the tools to be able to understand if they're suitable for your team and to help you scale your sales.

Using our process is a strategic approach that goes beyond simply looking at resumes, which is what most recruitment people are still doing.

Selling has only gotten harder and more difficult. Today's customers are empowered with endless options of information, and customers' journeys can be increasingly complex.

Corporate companies have invested in buyer training, and with the lack of investment in sales training, there's a 'Great Dividing Range' in cases (particularly with large buying groups) where you're dealing with a very talented buyer who has the volume and capacity to make some huge changes within your business. Some businesses struggle to recover from these changes.

For example, you may be the preferred supplier, which makes it easier for your sales team to get orders, but then you lose the contract. Then you're back to a completely different ball game.

Are your salespeople capable of winning new business opportunities or have they been riding on the back of your existing customers and existing contracts? This is a good question for you to answer. If you did lose a major contract, are you confident your team could create and win new business? From my experience, a high percentage would struggle.

What we want to do is make sure that you're fit for the fight, fit for 'finals football'.

We're now going to run through what this takes and how we do this and how we can help you select the best salespeople, using our crystal ball process.

Unfortunately, a lot of salespeople are in the under 50% sales percentile, so it's worth developing a strategy and nurturing those with potenial to be "elite" sellers.

Time is Money

As I mentioned in the introduction to this book, some people say you should hire slow and fire fast. I understand that thinking. But if you are hiring slow and someone else is doing it fast with more confidence backed by more science and data, then you are going to miss out.

Top sales candidates can get hired within days, so you do need to move relatively quickly. We have missed out on top talent because our clients have taken too long, they haven't decided on who should go through, and they have delayed the interview process.

Some candidates get annoyed, or they think, *"Is this what it's going to be like to work for them?"* And they'll take another role where the company is more efficient and transparent during the recruitment process.

For us, it's about the speed, but it's also about making sure that we are getting the best sales professionals for our clients. However, we have more data and information to back that speed up, and hopefully you will too in the future.

I'm going to give you a quick rundown on the sales DNA assessment tool. As highlighted in Chapter 6, it is sales-specific, predictive and 95% accurate.

Finding the Best Candidates

We put salespeople with relevant experience through to the assessment stage. They receive an automated email with an assessment link. It explains our process and that completion is required to progress. It takes approx. 45 mins, results straight to your inbox.

Assessment Recommendations and Status

You have three options:

1. **Not Recommended** (I'll start with the easy one.) The candidate hasn't met your criteria, or the sales DNA assessment criteria to proceed further. We formally reject them via an automated message.

2. **Worthy of Consideration**
    These candidates can potentially be shortlisted for further consideration if you don't have enough recommended candidates. Sometimes, a candidate might just miss out on a few parts or percentages of the criteria. For example, they could miss out by 3% on their sales DNA, not able to sell high-ticket items, or not able to sell to decision-makers—top "C-suite" executives.

3. **Recommended**
    These are candidates that you evaluate further. Now is the time to look further into their resume,

experience, job stability and other key areas that you require to succeed in your role. If they tick the boxes, we then move to an unbiased and structured phone call, followed by video or in-person interviews, as outlined in Chapter 6.

The assessment tool settings are customisable, so hiring managers can adjust them. For example, there is a toggle where we can ramp up the assessment difficulty of a role or soften it down to be a little bit easier.

It really depends on where you're at, the conditions of your marketplace that your salespeople are selling into, how competitive it is and any other dynamics of the role.

We do the process together, we share our knowledge, and we help you to make it easy to follow. It's critical to build criteria that reflect what it takes to succeed in your role. This helps you qualify early on who you should potentially be interviewing.

The Value of Using a Sales-Specific Assessment

I'm going to provide you with an example that demonstrates the value of uncovering the sales DNA of your existing team. Salespeople are like most of us. We can learn more, or if we're comfortable, we can end up with some bad habits and loss of motivation. The salesperson you hired, maybe years ago, might not be the same person now. Maybe the market you operated in or the role you hired them for has now changed and it's now turned into more of a hunting role. Maybe the salesperson isn't a fit anymore. And this takes me back to not just hiring for industry experience. Salespeople can change over time.

As an example, here is someone you don't want to hire, but many have:

- On paper, they have wide, product-related industry experience. The candidate that a lot would hire without any questions.
- But when we assessed them, they are in the bottom 23% of salespeople.

23 Sales Percentile	**NOT RECOMMENDED**	Meets OMG Criteria — No
		Meets Client Criteria — No

Will to Sell 39 Target 60	**Sales DNA** 49 Target 68	**Tactical** 35 Target 67

<table>
<tr><td>Desire</td><td>Doesn't Need Approval</td><td>Hunting</td></tr>
<tr><td>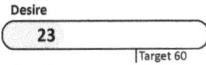 23 Target 60</td><td>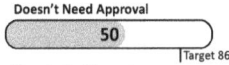 50 Target 86</td><td>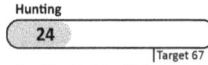 24 Target 67</td></tr>
<tr><td>Commitment</td><td>Stays in the Moment</td><td>Reaching Decision-Makers</td></tr>
<tr><td>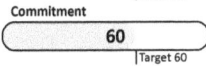 60 Target 60</td><td> 78 Target 88</td><td>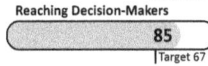 85 Target 67</td></tr>
<tr><td>Coachable</td><td>Supportive Beliefs</td><td>Relationship Building</td></tr>
<tr><td>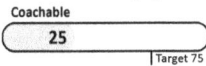 25 Target 75</td><td>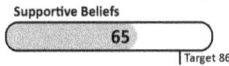 65 Target 86</td><td>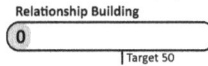 0 Target 50</td></tr>
<tr><td>Responsibility</td><td>Supportive Buy Cycle</td><td>Consulative Selling</td></tr>
<tr><td>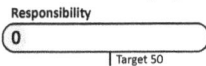 0 Target 50</td><td>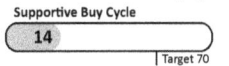 14 Target 70</td><td>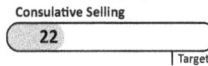 22 Target 80</td></tr>
<tr><td>Motivation</td><td>Comfortable Discussing Money</td><td>Selling Value</td></tr>
<tr><td>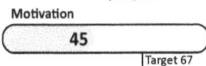 45 Target 67</td><td>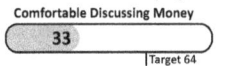 33 Target 64</td><td>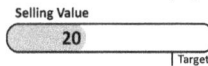 20 Target 80</td></tr>
</table>

Objective Management Group (OMG)

The assessment uncovered that this person had a lot of areas they were never going to change. I would rather know what someone can do and is not going to do BEFORE I hire them, otherwise it's too late.

The tool assesses **21 core competencies** across three main areas:

1. Will to sell.
2. Sales DNA. (Mindset)
3. Tactical selling skills.

The "will to sell" competency areas include **desire.** This salesperson doesn't dig deep; the assessment showed that they don't have persistence and "grit" to chase business. They are more comfortable doing "reactive" work. They won't do the hard yards to succeed. They take the easy road with less resistance.

Commitment is one of the other main competencies of "will to sell". A low score in commitment means that the candidate won't be committed to doing what's outside their comfort zone. They won't push hard, ask the tough questions and do the cold calls. They'll give up.

If there's pressure and if this person doesn't want to do anything that's outside their comfort zone, then it will be like a tug of war. They're going to be pulling back when you're trying to pull them forward. They're not going to move.

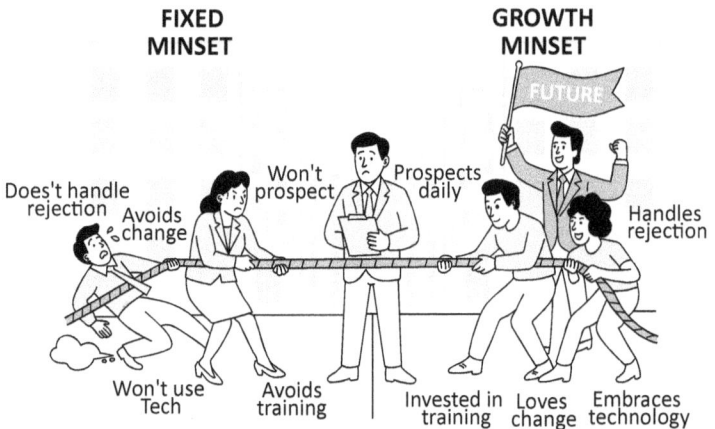

This person wasn't recommended, and I would never hire them. They don't take any **responsibility** for their actions. They blamed market conditions or pricing for their lack of success.

I'm just walking through some examples of the data we provide to our clients that is like giving them a crystal ball when it comes to recruiting and evaluating their current teams.

Our **mindset** can contain hidden roadblocks to success. Most of us in sales don't even know that these roadblocks exist. Unless we learn more about them, we will never get to the highest level. We coach a lot in this area. It can have a massive impact on success.

For example, if a salesperson needs to be liked, then they're not going to ask the difficult questions that they need to progress an opportunity if they won't push back.

Another key area of mindset is the ability to **stay in the moment.** Salespeople tend to have very active minds that are constantly ticking over and thinking about what they're going to say next.

Not being present in conversations erodes trust. Clients, like our partners, notice when you're distracted. Missing cues can derail important discussions. Listening builds credibility. It's crucial to stay focused, avoid self-centred talk, and let sales growth come from understanding—not just selling. Presence is a salesperson's most powerful tool.

Another mindset area that can help you select top sales performers is **supportive beliefs** or **supported buy cycle.**

"How we buy is how we sell."

Salespeople often sell the way they buy.

If they chase discounts or brag about negotiating hard, then they'll likely lead with price when selling. Likewise, if someone prefers space when shopping, they'll avoid pushing customers for an answer. I've seen this first-hand—how personal habits shape sales behaviour and impact customer trust. Salespeople need to understand this and how it's either contributing to or hindering their results. We do a lot of work in understanding what mindset they have.

Another key area is being comfortable discussing price. Price questions can help to speed up the sales process, so salespeople need to be comfortable asking price questions. For example:

- Would you mind sharing with me what price you're looking to pay or the price that you have been offered?

Then stay silent.

- Or is the pricing we've given you competitive compared to what you're currently paying?

Let them speak and listen to their answer. Don't jump in and put words in their mouth like a lot of salespeople do.

A lot won't even ask those questions because they're uncomfortable, but if they're not asking them, then the opportunity is probably going to go nowhere.

It will end in what I call a Mexican stand-off. Or worse still, the "ghost". They don't want to tell you the bad news, and you don't want to annoy them.

Let's move on to some of the **tactical** areas.

Our sample salesperson scored 35 out of a target of 67 in their tactical assessment, well below average. Add this on top of poor "will to sell" and low sales DNA scores, and this is where hiring on "industry experience" can bite you hard. Look, you might get 12 months out of the person, but you won't make an ROI. They will cost you money, you will soon have to start all over again.

From a **hunting** perspective, this person scored 24 against a target of 67. More than likely, they will be in reactive mode, customer-service, not pushing for growth.

If a salesperson is not confident to talk to a decision-maker, then more than likely they're dealing with people who are not making the decisions. They may be placing the orders, but at the end of the day, they are not making the buying decisions in a lot of cases.

Our sample salesperson also scored very low in **relationship-building**—the ability to build a relationship very early on in the sales process—with a score of 0 out of 50. This salesperson didn't want to be in this job; they weren't even interested in building a relationship. It was more about them, not helping.

You've no doubt seen it before. Salespeople who are there to pay the bills. There's no positive **sales posturing**, they're negative. In many cases, people don't want to talk to them.

Consultative selling—this salesperson's score here, 22! They don't listen, are not in the moment, don't ask open-ended questions, and don't understand how to progress a sale. They are self-absorbed. One CEO I know would say, "They're an oxygen thief." That person wasn't even going to see anyone. But that's another story.

Selling value—with a score of 20 out of 80, they were selling a high-end product! If you can't lead on value, well then all you can do is sell on price. It's one of the most critical areas to get people to sell on value and not just price.

From a **qualifying** perspective, this person had a score of 33. They really had no understanding of what a good client looked like, but they weren't prospecting anyway. They were simply taking enquiries—potentially wasting valuable time on people that would never order.

That leads me to their **closing** assessment score of zero. Yep! Zero. Now, this person has been in sales for over 15 years. But they shouldn't be in sales! They won't ask for the orders. Unfortunately, in our experience about two out of three salespeople don't! So, if you want to grow your business, a salesperson like that isn't going to do it.

I've always been the person that says, "Give me a quality sales professional any day who has the ability and the motivation to create and bring back new opportunities and win new business. It's easier to train somebody on products and industry, than teaching and motivating them to sell."

I've heard it all. "I don't have time to train them on our products…" Well, it's much easier to train for a product than for motivation and sales ability.

Now, one key area that we look at when we're doing the assessment is the confidence of how the person is answering the questions, whether they're taking a long time to think about them, and whether they're consistent with their answers.

Maybe they're answering the way they think they should instead of the way they would typically handle a sales enquiry or opportunity. If we think someone is trying it on, then we won't progress that candidate, because what else are they not going to do when they are working for you if they're trying to rort their assessment? It's not worth the risk from our experience. Our mission is for you to select the best sales professionals to progress.

The sales DNA assessment offers suggested interview questions so that you can drill down into areas of concern. It will even indicate potential answers that the candidate might come back with based on predictive data gathered from the tool having been used on over 2.8 million salespeople across the globe.[15]

Gaps in the 21 core competencies revealed by the assessment will impact the candidate's ability to win any major deals, unless they fall into their lap and they were going to get the order anyway.

This is what "good" looks like! A sales professional in the "top 15%".

85 Sales Percentile

RECOMMENDED

Meets OMG Criteria — Yes
Meets Client Criteria — Yes

Will to Sell	88 Target 60	Sales DNA	85 Target 68	Tactical	72 Target 67
Desire	93 Target 60	Doesn't Need Approval	75 Target 86	Hunting	100 Target 67
Commitment	80 Target 60	Stays in the Moment	89 Target 88	Reaching Decision-Makers	35 Target 67
Coachable	100 Target 75	Supportive Beliefs	89 Target 86	Relationship Building	54 Target 50
Responsibility	100 Target 50	Supportive Buy Cycle	71 Target 70	Consulative Selling	80 Target 80
Motivation	85 Target 67	Comfortable Discussing Money	100 Target 64	Selling Value	91 Target 80

Objective Management Group (OMG)

Quick Selection Tips:

- Use automation to acknowledge each application quickly.
- Set clear expectations about recruitment timelines and steps right from the outset.

- Remove any administrative barriers throughout your recruitment process.
- Don't let AI replace human conversations.
- Streamline the process to a maximum of three interviews when you use the assessment tool to provide you with hard data to support your hiring decision.

Interviewing Stage

Firstly, you don't want to be interviewing too many people. I know some hiring managers that have interviewed 10 people for an hour each or longer. We interview less people, and our process is short and sweet, because we've already found out much more information from their sales DNA assessment than from simply reading a resume.

- **Step 1: 5-minute phone call**

    The goal for the first phone call is to set expectations. We talk about experience versus criteria to see whether the candidate meets the requirements, we talk a little bit about the expertise you're looking for. We learn how familiar the candidate is with the market you sell into, and whether they know much about your business. Would you want them representing your company? Did they show some sort of commitment to taking the next step?

We push back a little bit to see how they handle it. They're going to get objections, so we see how they go. It could be something that stood out from their assessment results that concerned you.

If the phone screen goes well and you believe they could be a good fit for an interview, then while you have them on the phone, lock in a time for a video interview that will be recorded. Do it ASAP. We like to do it within a few days. Don't wait too long.

- **Step 2: Recorded video interview (15 minutes)**

If you're going solo and using your sales DNA results, then you've got so much data to work with to prepare for your interview. I ensure that I have the results open, along with the candidate's resume so that I can cross-reference.

One of the most important things to do when you're interviewing is to let the candidate attempt to build rapport. Don't make it too easy for them. Maybe they have looked at your LinkedIn profile, connected with you or they've looked at your website. They should have!

Check out their warmth and the tonality of their voice. Are they friendly? Are they loud and abrasive, or are they timid and uncomfortable?

Some people can get nervous in an interview, but you can also get nervous when you are walking into a new prospect or seeing a new client that you want to do new business with. Evaluate whether:

- They speak clearly, concisely and with authority.
- They communicate their ideas effectively.
- They have a personal presence.

Is this person you would choose to listen to and again, is this someone that you would like to represent your company?

To throw them off guard a little, say, "We're not sure whether you're a good fit for the role." How do they come back?

Here are some questions that we use to dig deeper into a candidate's ability that can be leveraged during your reference checks. These are just a guide, but remember, agree on the questions, and keep them consistent to remove any bias:

- If it's BDM position, explain that it's a "heavy hunting" role. "Are you committed to doing this every day?" You must hear a positive answer, and it will help later if they're hired and push back.
- "What motivates you to sell more?" (Compare their answer to their sales DNA assessment).
- "What are your career goals?" You want to make sure they align with your company's.
- "Tell us about a major project you successfully won. How did you do it?

- "If we asked your recent bosses, which we will do if we progress to reference checks, what would they rate your performance on a scale of 1–10 (with 10 being the highest)?" You're looking for 8s or 9s.

If we're recruiting for you, at this stage we still haven't presented any candidates, because we only want to present the top 20%. It depends how you prefer to work. Some clients like to see a candidate's profile before we interview them. Others don't.

Our theory is that the best use of time is to get the right candidates with the right results and the right experience, then show you a 15-minute recorded video interview with them. Some of our clients love it because they can watch the interview in their own time and have other team members watch it as well.

- **Step 3: Second interview and negotiations**

    When we work with most of our clients, we hand it over to you after the first video interview to conduct second interviews if required to negotiate compensation and other arrangements. Or we can do your reference checks and negotiation if required. Or, if you're hiring in-house, we're here to consult and support you in any required areas. Our options are flexible.

    (In chapter 10, you'll learn more about how you can become STAR™ accredited and recruit like an expert.

You'll receive full access to all the documentation, systems and processes to support your hiring team.)

As outlined in Chapter 6, use a scorecard to evaluate their answers to your structured interview questions. You should also evaluate how much they spoke compared to how much you spoke. Most platforms will now provide this data for video interviews.

To finish up, if you're confident that a candidate will progress, let them know that they'll be expected to organise recent bosses or colleagues (preferably someone they've reported to) for reference checks. Too many times, we see candidates select a friend or someone that will help them exit a company to make their problem go away. You don't want to inherit this person if that's the case. Now is your time to avoid that trouble.

Let me share one of our many success stories. This was the first role we were recruiting for a particular client. One of the hiring team members was focused on hiring a candidate with both product and industry experience (a bias). This person was adamant that they didn't have the time or the systems and processes to train for product experience.

Thankfully, the CEO was open to a wider search. The best candidate we found did not have relevant experience, but they had some knowledge of the industry. Our assessment determined that the candidate had a strong growth mindset, tactical skills and the sales ability to fill a gap this company had in getting out there and effectively targeting to grow new business. This candidate was hired and went on to be one of the company's best performers.

This is where our crystal ball comes into play. It will feed you the right information. Our mission is to bring the best sales talent to our clients. We've seen success like doubling the sales of a company to turn it from a low-level competitor into a major industry innovator and leader.

It can happen, but you need to have the right people in the right role. It's a blend, like a fine soup. Add the right ingredients and it will taste better.

If you haven't worked it out by now, we're a big process and structured flow company. We love to see processes and structures created and then we love to see successful hire stories unfold. Unfortunately, we see the missed critical steps of companies that try to jump ahead with their recruitment process. Move through our process and it will reward you.

It's going to take longer the first time, but once you've done it a few times, you'll understand and see the benefits. Hiring sales talent is a mixture of art and science. Once you master this, scaling large teams will be much easier.

I've seen company growth stall because they're not confident of the talent they can attract to drive their growth. If you're a startup and you get your first sales hire wrong, then it could be the end of your business. I've seen it happen.

HOW TO SELECT THE BEST TALENT

You must have the best person to start with in terms of ability, and they need the systems and processes to be successful. When you engage us to support your hiring process, we need to make sure you are ready to guarantee success. We've seen it too many times when new salespeople are set up to fail. It doesn't help anyone.

If you're an expert in your field, but not at recruiting, then get expert help from us. We can be on your side. We can do as much or as little as you want, from candidate screening and unbiased assessment through to interviewing, reference checking, making offers, negotiating contracts, hiring, onboarding, and the workshop training for your hiring team.

We will ensure that you don't invest your valuable time into interviewing candidates who don't meet your criteria or won't do what you want them to do and or get you the results that you deserve. You deserve salespeople that are going to make you money, not cost you money. This is not a free ride.

Get expert help like we do in our business. We have a great accountant, and they do their job, because it's not my specialty.

If you're reading this book, we'd love to work with you. We understand how difficult it is to attract and find top sales talent. We know how tough it is looking after HR across business services and systems. We want your future salespeople to be successful and for them to hit the ground running.

Remember my story from earlier in the book about driving down the highway when a salesperson is not performing. Visualise $100 bills flying out the window with every kilometre they go, every hotel they stay in, every expenditure they put in for a lunch with someone that probably wasn't the right person. These are all added costs.

When I started my business (Arrow Executive Sales) I was looking for a purple cow like the concept described in Seth Godin's book that I explained in the Introduction of this book. If you haven't read it, do so. It's an easy and short read, but it's a powerful message. Hopefully, like this book is.

A purple cow is doing something that's different from what everyone else is doing. There is a huge sales recruitment problem that needs to change, and if I didn't become accredited, invest in my own training and development, and use the assessment tool, then it would be difficult for me to find the best talent for my business or those of my clients. I'd be no different to other recruiters.

We continue to push the boundaries of best sales recruitment practice. We don't stop. How far can we push to deliver the best?

We want the best salespeople for you. The top 10% or 20%. We also want this sales professional to stay in your business, but only if they're performing.

From one of our clients:
"Once Arrow stepped in, the process became efficient and effective. We started with one hire who hit the ground running and delivered a massive ROI."

"Then came the second, third, and now the fourth BDM— all within six months. Each hire feels stronger than the last."

"It's not just about getting people in—it's about getting the right people. And every time, we're refining that fit."

We're always investing in new technology. We're always practising. We're students of the craft of sales and recruitment.

You never stop learning. So hopefully you're learning from this book.

CHAPTER 8

Onboarding for Success

Onboarding is a critical area that is often quite underestimated and undervalued. I think back to my own time as a sales leader, it wasn't until the end of my tenure that I came across a quality HR manager who presented me with an onboarding process and I was like, "Wow". It was incredible.

Some people are lucky to have a great HR leader, some people don't get anyone, some people must do it themselves.

I've heard many salespeople blamed for not making the grade. But it's a two-way street and we see both sides.

It's like Halloween. I'll share some things in this chapter that will shock you. But I'll also share some information that will help you hopefully build a new onboarding program or you can use ours to have more success with your hiring.

Recent research shows that 47% of sales executives have left a sales job due to poor onboarding or training.[16] 70% of new hires also say that their job was misrepresented to them.[17]

The biggest issues we find when onboarding is done poorly is the lack of clarity and direction. New hires feel lost. They're unsure of their priorities or how success is measured. It also leads to potential disengagement and early turnover. We see a lot of that.

It could be due to information overload—dumping too much too fast or failing to provide enough context so that it's not confusing. It could also be due to limited (or no) engagement from their manager who is wearing too many hats.

Leaders can also assume that HR or other people are handling the onboarding. Without sales leadership involvement in onboarding, you will struggle for alignment and motivation within the team.

Critical Failure Points to Avoid

Here are critical failure points for sales onboarding in most companies:

- **They don't really have an onboarding process.**
It's not built into or integrated into their technology so that it can be followed and managed to ensure that every new hire goes through the same experience.

In a lot of examples we see, the onboarding is more about just product training onboarding for a few days. The standard process often involves simply receiving a phone, a set of keys and maybe a product manual before being sent out to see customers typically within two or three days. Salespeople who are not prepared are out seeing customers.

This is very much a 'learn as you go' approach. It's a little bit of a hit and hope, with the salesperson rarely even receiving a customer rundown call sheet. Here's an example: I know a gentleman, let's call him Larry, who is a good-quality sales professional. He has worked at several businesses across our industry. I had the privilege of catching up with Larry recently in Brisbane for a cold beer and a bit of a fireside chat.

I asked him about his onboarding experiences across different companies, and he said it was "poor".

Most companies he's worked for didn't have an onboarding program except for one. He had a highly structured, week-long induction at Bunnings which covered its company culture, policies and operational aspects. There were no hidden surprises with one of Australia's biggest retailers, and one of my clients for nearly 16 years.

Bunnings has a brilliant culture. I always love going to the stores. You see a lot of passion. You see a lot of energy, and sometimes the staff members wear the apron with pride.

- **Their onboarding process isn't aligned with their sales strategy.**

Don't be surprised, but there are still companies that don't have a strategy, or if they do, then it's not clearly reflected to the team or the individual salespeople.

If your onboarding process doesn't reflect the go-to market strategy or your buyer's journey and process, then what you can find is that new reps waste a lot of time on outdated tactics, irrelevant messaging or chasing the wrong types of prospects.

- **They are set up for failure without realising it.**

Right now, if you look at the landscape according to the Australian HR Institute's 2022 Report, line managers in 47% of organisations are responsible for much of the HR function, especially in smaller or leaner companies.[18]

Breaking this down by business size:

- **Small business 1 to 19 employees**

Typically, they have no dedicated HR team. Recruiting and onboarding is typically handled by the hiring manager or business owner. Processes are usually very informal and often not documented, relying on the person delivering the onboarding to do it properly.

There is also more than likely no (or very limited) use of onboarding software. Or automation, even now in 2025.

If you look at their style of onboarding, it's very personalised and ad hoc, but lacks the consistency of delivery. It's clunky.

Most hires are fast-tracked and expected to contribute quickly, and limited training is provided in a high percentage of situations. You may get some shadowing. Maybe some verbal instructions, if you're lucky.

Being an inconsistent experience, with more hiring managers across multiple locations with different skill sets and patience levels, the risk is high when issues arise with compliance. With a lack of formal documentation, there are also liability concerns.

It places a very high expectation on the manager doing the onboarding who generally is busy working on other things as well.

- **Medium business, 20 to 199 employees**
They are likely to have a HR team. From my experience, once a company gets to about 50, you would tend to integrate a HR manager or a HR service provider into the business. But again, all companies are different, and HR can tend to get heavily involved in daily duties, leaving not a lot of time to recruit salespeople.

When I was in my national sales role and growing a sales team, we relied on previous documentation. We did our own onboarding process, and did all the hiring, and I made a lot of mistakes. I take full ownership of that and didn't realise how difficult it is.

In medium-sized businesses, you may get some better onboarding and formal documentation. They tend to use basic HR software.

If you look at the onboarding style, it could include a checklist, a small welcome pack and some scheduled training. It might have a mix of in-person and or digital onboarding, and it could be tailored to departments or job functions with role-specific onboarding. Depending on the industry, the size of company within the bracket, and its leadership, onboarding styles can vary quite dramatically.

- **Large business of 200+ employees**
They should have dedicated HR departments and a comprehensive onboarding program often spanning for weeks or even months.

From my experience in dealing with companies of this size and recruiting through their HR departments, sometimes they're busy hiring for every role within the business, and a sales position is done in conjunction with a sales manager. From an onboarding perspective, typically it is highly structured and standardised, but it can vary in different industries.

Some companies work on a multi-phase onboarding process that even covers pre-boarding, before they start technology integration and/or ongoing development.

You can also look at involvement from IT payroll and different people from within the business. However, it can still be a challenge maintaining engagement at a personal level when coordinating across multiple departments and locations. A higher percentage of leaders right now are wearing multiple hats, so ensuring alignment with company culture and values can be challenging.

Every situation is different. For example, I'd noticed a lot of jobs advertised by a particular company on Seek, which can be a good sign of a company that is growing, but beware, it can also be a sign of churning due to leadership and culture issues.

I reached out to the leader to find out. What I discovered isn't uncommon. They're quite a large company with multiple locations around the country. And each branch manager is responsible for their own hiring. We're talking about 15 sites, so that's 15 different managers hiring, and they have limited HR support.

None of them have ever been trained how to recruit, either. They are also quite desperate to get people on the ground, so there are no effective recruitment processes and no training.

I saw some of the people who they had recruited. Many had been through our assessment process for our clients, and they had scored in the bottom half of salespeople. It wasn't their fault. Looking through their resumes, several companies they'd previously worked are renowned for not investing in training or development. This is where not investing can hurt, and bad...

The people this company had hired were, at best, very average salespeople. Some were in our bottom 30%. It does prove that not all the big companies or the industry-leading ones that you'd expect to be on top of their recruitment are on top of it.

When you look at HR involvement overall, it's generally non-existent or very minimal for small businesses, moderate for medium businesses and high for large businesses. And, in terms of the amount of time spent on onboarding, it is usually short for small businesses, moderate for medium businesses and longer for a large business.

HR is responsible for the broader function of recruitment and other day-to-day HR activities. Typically, HR people do require some sort of training to hire salespeople, as sales requires specific skills like persuading candidates and understanding the sales industry. While HR will focus on cultural alignment and compliance, they often need support from sales leadership or specialised recruiters to build a strong, sales-focused talent pool and profile, and to conduct effective interviews. Teamwork in recruitment is good.

With many of our clients, if their HR manager has a lot going on, or they've had trouble attracting candidates, they've brought us in to help them in that role. Or we provide the tools to support their hiring decisions.

What Good Onboarding Looks Like

It wasn't until my final years of sales leadership that a quality HR professional showed me what best practice looked like for onboarding. If you're working for a company with a HR manager, then you might have been more fortunate.

To understand your onboarding process in more detail, you've got to look at the scoreboard to see what's worked for you in the past, what hasn't, and what needs to change. It's an ongoing process.

Firms like IBM and Hewlett Packard were known for being hugely successful at onboarding, offering a full year of training before sales quotas were assigned. It earned them reputations as a top destination for sales employees.[19]

Sales staff must know their product, the market, and their ideal clients. It's not just about explaining features—it's about understanding segments, using the right techniques and technology, and anticipating objections before they arise. Great salespeople prepare, adapt, and handle resistance with confidence and clarity.

By investing in comprehensive onboarding, training and coaching, organisations can set their sales members up to succeed from the start.

Avoid just doing paperwork on day one. Start building internal relationships, show them around, take them on some tours and talk to other people.

Here are some typical onboarding topics:

- Company history
- Organisational structure
- Reporting structure

- Product training
- CRM certification and training
- Value propositions and messaging
- Marketplace dynamics and where your company and product are positioned
- A SWOT analysis of the competitive landscape
- Where your pricing strategy sits
- Sales results over the last few years, and forecasts
- Statistics for sales cycles
- Your territory planning and sales calling volumes
- CRM reporting expectations
- Pre-sales call preparation
- Communication templates for consistency and time-saving
- What a typical sales call looks like
- What a typical prospecting call looks like
- How long it should be before they generate some business.

If you are onboarding a new sales manager, then onboard them as if they were a new salesperson initially to give them a first-hand understanding of the sales process and the team dynamics.

Good onboarding could involve having a buddy. I like this system, but make sure you pick the right one. I've seen it backflip with negative or disruptive "buddies" ruining new hires within days.

I had a couple of buddies when I was at Hyne. They helped me build confidence. It accelerated my learning, and it fostered good connections within the business. You know who you are. Thank you.

Good onboarding should involve co-calling some of your top accounts with other top salespeople. It helps to build trust and a sense of belonging.

Setting Early Performance Objectives

Setting early performance objectives can help you to gauge the effectiveness of your recruitment and onboarding processes. It can also help you to identify further training needs.

Here are some example early performance objectives for a sales rep:

- To be able to resolve 90% of inbound calls within four to five minutes, after week 2.
- Help them to log into your CRM and other sales technology. To be able to search for client information, past interactions, and areas to follow up on from the last salesperson, after week 1.
- Submitting call planners and reports, on a weekly basis when on the road.
- Reach budget within four months after satisfactory completion of a 30-day onboarding/training program.
- Conduct a successful discovery call to understand the root causes of existing client problems to help

them prospect for new business more effectively. Potentially within nine months, this person could be an established hunter who is targeting new business and qualifying to earn commissions.

The first 90 days are make-or-break moments. You really want to be able to tick off some boxes with your new hires. Make sure they can identify an ideal client profile so that they are hunting in the right areas in the future. It's very important to make sure that they're targeting the right people.

Make yourself available for 1:1 coaching each week. It might only need to be for 15 or 20 minutes, but be there for your new hires. Schedule the time in before anything goes pear- shaped, so you can work through it much more effectively together. Coach your sales style—your approach to selling—from identifying prospects to closing new business. If they're a hunter or a farmer, look at specific training to help them. We can help with that if you're interested.

You want your new people to be comfortable within your business from day one that they've joined a very professional company. Show confidence in new hires by planting them on fertile ground with good seedlings that can develop into major and mature plants, then help them manage that mix. Asking a new salesperson to open a new territory is a recipe for failure. Move accounts around between your team so that they are assigned in a balanced way.

Ideally, have a top five target list of potential prospects for your new salesperson so they're not starting from scratch. We have an **ideal client profile** template within our onboarding process. This is a great way to kick off onboarding, instead of making them start all over again.

Assessment, Onboarding and Training

As I've said throughout this book, hiring a salesperson is a big investment (typically $200,000 per annum). It's crucial to get your hiring, onboarding and ongoing training right. If you use the sales DNA assessment tool as part of both your recruitment process and the evaluation of your existing team, then you will know the level and type of training that is needed for each person.

Humans aren't machines. We're all different. We all have different mindsets, experience, knowledge and levels of sales success, so unless you use our 'crystal ball' processes, you won't readily know all this information. You'll be on guessing.

I always relate onboarding and training back to 10-pin bowling with kids—guardrails and ramps help to guide the ball. In sales, your processes and systems do the same. More structure means faster, more consistent onboarding—and a chance to teach your unique sales approach.

Great salespeople aren't born; they're hired or built!

Think of these potential hiring situations:

1. **You hired a sales A-player who knows your industry and clients.**
   Remember that each company is unique. Different market share, culture, strategies and leadership. It doesn't mean this person is necessarily going to succeed in your business. They still require a strong onboarding program.

2. **You hired a salesperson who didn't quite tick all the boxes but who was your best option to recruit from a limited talent pool.**
   This happens a lot. You can hope that they work out or you can invest in improving their abilities to increase the likelihood that they will. If you have used the sales DNA assessment tool, then at least you know where they need mentoring or training to help them ramp up quicker and improve their sales performance. Providing a mentor or scheduling specific sales training in those areas will provide a higher chance of success.

   This can be the difference between success and being back out there rehiring in another three to six months, not to mention the negative impact on your sales team when new hires don't work out.

3. **You hired a salesperson who is missing more boxes than they ticked.**
   Maybe they are from within your business in another role. You know them, but you'd nearly

bet that they won't make it. I've seen this happen many times before. You're directed to give them a go, but you know it could really hurt! It will likely create more work and put more pressure on you. Unfortunately, you could be blamed if it doesn't work, so give it your best shot early in your process.

How Much to Invest for Onboarding and Training

Best practice is to invest 5% of a salesperson's annual remuneration for onboarding and training. Think of it like insurance or servicing your car. If you don't invest in servicing your car and changing your oil, then you could risk blowing your engine up.

It's a similar concept with onboarding and training your salespeople. Invest in them to make sure that they're tuned up to perform. It will pay off tenfold. If you don't and you wing it instead, then there's a fair chance that they will fail. If this continues, then the finger could potentially be pointed back in your direction.

Sales skills consistently evolve, so continuously train your team. If you look at doctors and lawyers, they're consistently undertaking education. And builders, they've got to get their points. They have no choice, it's regulated. Professionals must do the same thing.

Key Takeaways

Consider these statistics:
- Companies with effective onboarding programs see 73% higher budget attainment rates.
- Structured onboarding programs are 15 times more likely to generate new business opportunities.
- Structured onboarding programs result in 54% more productivity from new hires.
- Salespeople who undergo robust onboarding are 18 times more committed to the organisation and have an average tenure of 3 years + (double the average).
- 25% of sales hires quit within their first year, often saying lack of structure or support. There is a huge turnover cost that includes lost potential revenue and ramp-up times that are an average 5.3 months for new hires.[20]

You can also download more information online via the following QR code or by visiting: www.jasonhowes.com.au/books/downloads.

CHAPTER 9

Retaining Your Top Performers

It's difficult to find quality sales professionals, let alone retain them. It's a full-time job to retain top performers, but the rewards they provide make it worthwhile.

To retain top sales talent, you need to focus on creating a positive and supportive work culture and environment where they want to work. You want to be known in the industry as the place to work. To do this, you must lead with vision, clarity, and support.

You must consistently be there in the moment for your top performers and your team. For example, by understanding what's happening in their life and how they are feeling. Be a good listener and it will help you retain your top performers. They deserve to be heard.

Additionally, it's crucial to ensure that you clearly communicate, and that you have transparency and a lot of trust. I've experienced a lack of communication and transparency. I've seen closed doors, not knowing what's going on, secrecy, politics and all those things. That is not a place to retain top performers.

You want to make sure that your top performers enjoy where they are. Remember that the average tenure of a salesperson is just 18 months. If you have those stats for your top performers, they create a very costly cycle for your business. Even worse, if you have a very long sales cycle (for example, you're involved in specifications for large projects that can take years), then the salesperson who started the project potentially won't be there to close the sale!

In a lot of situations, the turnover is so rapid that the return on investment is not there at all.

People are typically not ramping up. A good sales professional can ramp up in three to six months. If they're average, they might take 12 months, if at all! If you look at an average salesperson tenure of 18 months, then if you're taking over 12 months to ramp them up, you're not making a return on investment during that time.

Today's leaders must become experts in managing top performers. It's critical to see the importance from a leadership perspective, and that's why many say that a sales manager should be available to coach their team 50% of the time. That's best practice.

However, it would be fair to say that we don't ever see this with companies we work with.

Coaching time includes weekly 1:1's. That might seem like a lot if you have a team of 10, but each 1:1 might only need to be for 15 to 20 minutes. Regular contact with your top performers is critical. Don't get caught up spending most of your time with underperformers. That's a trap.

Employee Value Proposition

First, you need to have an employee value proposition that defines the uniqueness or the promise that you make to employees regarding their experience and the benefits that they expect to receive. Leaders must walk the walk. You can't just talk the talk.

If you're promising a good culture and experience, then you must deliver on that. Consistently. And it's challenging.

Otherwise, your top performers will walk out the door. And we've seen that just recently. Top performers will move on. They get other jobs with ease. And it's not always about the money.

Effective value propositions typically revolve around four components:

- Number one, is the company. Its purpose, values and culture.

- Then comes leadership and relationships with managers.
- Then the role and the actual job that they're doing with opportunities for development.
- And finally, the rewards, including benefits and things like work-life balance.

And some of these components are overlooked by many companies. Your first job is to determine the cultural values that make your organisation stand out as the best place to work. If you can't come up with those, then that could be a problem. It could be why you're losing people.

If you are losing top performers, then you also need to understand what you promised versus what you delivered. Now is a good time to reflect:

- Have you stood up to our promise?
- If you haven't, then why, and what needs to change?

Because when you've experienced a top performer walking out of the door, it's not good. I'm not talking about someone that's simply walked in and had all the good customers and looks like a great performer. I'm talking about someone who has won new business opportunities, grown your sales or taken your company to the next level.

Before you jump into combat mode of offering more money when a salesperson lets you know they want to leave, consider whether they have been a high performer. Pull back the covers and review their numbers. Look in your CRM, what are their activity levels like? Or, potentially like their calendar, is it empty? Is there a pipeline full of opportunities that they are progressing? If it isn't looking positive, then potentially they left the building a long time ago.

Good hiring based on high-performance core values is critical. As a hiring manager and leader, we must structure our hiring process to ensure recruits will fit. Simply hiring someone from a competitor can upset the apple cart. You could pay more money to get them, with no guarantee that they will perform unless you use the sales DNA assessment to hire for competencies and strength instead, not just apparent skills and experience.

Leaders should inspire their salespeople. They should coach and build confidence within their team. If a top performer has lost confidence with their team, then they're probably going to go somewhere else. You're not going to retain them.

In addition, consider whether you supply your top performers with the best tools of the trade. For example, automated technology that will save them time and effort when sitting in the car and filling in CRM information, so that they can spend their time on more valuable tasks.

Ask your salespeople these questions to help them do their job more effectively:

- What do you need to save you time?
- What do you need to be able to close more deals?

Get them out of their normal environment to find out. My old boss used to ask these questions over a bite to eat. I got a lot of value from it. Salespeople need to feel valued. We've seen it quite often where a business will spend money on luxury cars, operations and new sites. And their salespeople are out there, quite often, underequipped and undervalued.

Transparent Compensation

It's critical to understand that the recognition and rewards for our salespeople and their achievements and contributions go a long way to boosting and supporting their morale and their motivation.

You want to be able to celebrate success by providing incentives and opportunities to acknowledge their individual and team efforts that will help create a positive and encouraging environment to grow as a team.

Are your rewards attractive enough to retain your top performers? We spoke about that in Chapter 4.

For top performers, you want to make sure that your remuneration is above current industry standards. Don't leave the door open for your competitors! Trust me, it will cost you far more if they leave and you have to replace them.

In addition, are your incentives achievable? If you're not paying any commissions, especially for top performers, then something's wrong. It's either your people, your systems, your processes, or your incentives are not accurate or reflective of market conditions. It's time to regroup, and quickly. Many times, I've seen promises from leaders that they're "rebuilding" incentives schemes, only to postpone it typically because they're not sure how to build one that works. It's not easy.

If salespeople need more money to survive and pay the mortgage, then it can force them to look around. Or maybe someone will approach them at the right time. If that happens to one of your top performers, then it will be a problem unless your current compensation and benefits offering is competitive.

Recognise and reward fairly and clearly. If you're not paying any incentives and your team is not meeting budget, then it's likely you're not going to get paid your incentive either. If you are, then the alignment is out. This is also why I also like to develop leading KPIs that contribute to rewarding your team for doing the right activities that drive results in line with your strategic plan.

You do get what you pay for. "Pay peanuts, you get monkeys," my old boss Peter Dallimore said.

Ensure They're in the Right Role

Are your top performers in the right role now? Not just to suit you, but them. This is quite often a problem.

Maybe they've been moved into a leadership or a sales management role, but maybe that's not the right role for them.

Try asking them. You could hear this response: "Not really, I preferred my old position. I only took the new role because I wanted more money. Or a better car."

Do you understand what motivates them? What goals do they have, and are those goals aligned? Did they set them, or you?

We want to make sure our top performers are doing what they love doing the most to fill their tank.

Here's an example. I visited a factory one day. This guy loved what he did. I said, "What do you love about working here? You're passionate."

And he goes, "You know what? The owner's great. He knows I love fishing, and he gives me every Friday off to go fishing. I take the boat out. I do four big days. It works for me."

And these are the little things you can do.

Handling Resignations

"I'm going to resign," or "Here's my resignation." You really don't want to hear these words. Potentially, the person saying them could just be testing the water. If you've just recruited a new hire or given someone a promotion and word is out that they got a good package, then this is where your close relationship that you've worked on with your top performer via open and transparent communication will pay off.

Ask why. And listen, don't put words in their mouth, like "Is it money?" Maybe they're in debt or struggling with work-life balance. Quite often, job travel can be an issue. You want to hear the reason from them.

Remember to be in the moment by being a good listener. Hear them out. Maybe they need a good mentor? Someone to get things aligned again. Or some time off? Ask them if a week's paid leave would assist them? It's cheaper than replacing someone.

I recommend that you always set a follow-up meeting. Lock in a time, don't just let them walk away into the wilderness. Show them you care.

It's also a good opportunity to make sure they're still as good as you thought. People can change. Nobody is irreplaceable, but it does also depend on how prepared you are. You may feel like you can get someone better now that you have access to *Crystal Ball Recruiting*.

Develop Career Trajectories

Maybe they're looking for a new challenge, a project you can both work on together. How can they get to the next level? You want to provide opportunities for growth and development.

We're working with clients to develop a career trajectory for their teams. For example, "If I'm working as an account manager, where can I go next?" Maybe it's a BDM position, then a sales manager, then key accounts or national sales manager.

It's about retaining your top performers. Giving them that vision that there is career growth potential in staying.

If you tick all the boxes and something pops up, and they're talking about leaving or they get approached, then you're able to retain them because you have made it so good with your business that they don't want to leave. They see a future.

With the high price of replacing salespeople, it's hard to believe that many companies just think that retention is too hard. Annual reviews don't work, if you're relying solely on this, think again.

In this changing environment, and we see this with some of companies that we hire for, they're focused on hiring better people when they also need to focus more on their succession planning and holding their top performers.

We talk about investing in your people through helping them develop new skills through study or mentoring. Ensuring they've got a clear pathway. We see this with a lot of top sales professionals. They've done a lot of investment in their professional development because their companies have put them through it. They've supported their top performers' growth, and they are rewarded with their loyalty.

Try giving your employees more ownership over their career path. Start a conversation with them about possibilities for learning, career growth and transformation right from the get-go. Allocated funds into compensation packages, and 5% towards professional development per annum to ensure they're always learning and bringing new skills to your business.

Make it part of your onboarding program, and once they've met probation or achieved consistently high results, then move into a plan of how you can help them.

For example, give them an opportunity to assist with a new hire. One of our clients brings in his salespeople to interview new team members. He wants them to be involved, to talk about what it's like to work in their company, and to also ensure that his bias doesn't lean the wrong way.

Let them be a buddy for new recruits to help with onboarding. This shows your top performers that they're valued within your business. For new product development, involve your top salespeople to show your appreciation. And you want to enable them to provide feedback.

What we want to do is build a culture that values balance and belonging, as well as a culture of appreciation and recognition for salespeople. Build that culture because you want to make sure that your top salespeople are engaged in meaningful work to help you retain your team.

Salespeople thrive when leaders set expectations, remove roadblocks, provide support and listen to where they're at. For example, providing a healthy work-life balance with their family, health and the flexibility to do what they love.

Empowerment

Empowerment is about having the clarity in structure to work independently and oversee your own output. Are your top performers' direct managers suitable? Do they respect and trust their leader?

A major reason why a lot of performers leave is because they don't trust and respect their direct manager. And you don't want that. Unfortunately, recent research shows that 82% of companies choose the wrong managers.[21]

I look back to some of my past jobs, and I was fortunate I love to play competitive squash and played a high level, the top 5% in Brisbane. Practice was super important, and some mornings at 6 a.m. I'd train. Or after work, sometimes at four or five in the afternoon. When I was travelling a lot, sometimes 2–3 times a month interstate, I struggled to fit this in. But my bosses always knew that I was working, putting in the hours, so they gave me that flexibility.

It gave me a sharper mindset. It kept me fit.

Great leaders set the expectations and know what needs to happen, they provide support when required.

If we won a big contract and we needed product, then they removed the roadblocks and made it happen. They were there as a mentor, and would offer advice and he helped me to navigate the challenges.

My job was to lead the sales team, and I was provided with the opportunity to do that.

Maybe one of your managers is a lone wolf? It could be that they aren't a good listener or aren't really a team player. Not every person is meant to be a manager. It isn't easy, especially that most haven't been trained.

Customer Satisfaction

If you've got a happy and engaged salesperson backed by high-quality customer service, then this will help you to retain your salespeople.

Supply, service or people issues can have a negative effect on salespeople, especially if they're not being heard. For example, they could have a stubborn operations manager or customer service manager who doesn't want to take responsibility for an issue.

We saw that during COVID where many companies struggled with stock. Suddenly, everyone was being let down. This wasn't unusual, but some salespeople left. They became more like counsellors, consistently having to deliver bad news. I've been there before; it can wear you down. But it's also part of the job.

And in some cases, these people who left probably jumped the gun and left jobs they once loved.

This is where you want to get feedback and create an environment where people can have their voice and be heard. If that's gone, you will see your top performers walk out the door.

Managerial Challenges

Quality talent quite often leaves because of poor managers. The common trap we see in a lot of companies is that they will promote workers into a managerial position because they feel like they should, or they feel like it's easier or they feel like they deserve it.

But at the end of the day, sometimes what you're doing is taking someone away from a position where they might be doing okay into a position where they struggle, and then they get performance-managed out. They either can't go back to the other role because of their pride, or they don't want to. And then suddenly, you've lost a good person because they were promoted to the wrong role.

Experience and skills are important, but people's talents are naturally recurring patterns in the way they think, feel and behave. They predict where they'll perform at their best. You want to get the right people in the right role.

Gallup research shows that only one in 10 people possesses an inherent talent to manage.[22] When you do the maths for a team of ten, it's likely that someone on each team has a talent to lead, but chances are that it's not the manager!

In a lot of cases, people get a managerial job because they are a family member, someone's mate, or because they say the right things. I know I've said this a lot, but potentially they may get promoted simply because they had the best accounts when they were selling.

The managerial talent pool is shrinking, and companies are really struggling. The quality gap in managers is huge. Whether this is a site/branch manager. Maybe they've been trained to manage operations, but not sales. That is completely different.

Often, they're expected to do both, and I rarely see it work. One of the largest battles we see our clients face is when there is no dedicated sales manager. As an example, I'll refer to a team of between 2–5. The business owner or manager is either the sales manager or they will pass that responsibility onto a salesperson to both service customers and manage the team. Let's also add in that they're recruiting salespeople as well, again having never been trained how to recruit. It's a disaster waiting to happen, which costs companies millions in lost revenue.

However, this is where strategic clarity emerges from uncertainty with our *Crystal Ball Recruiting.*

If you read Jim Collins' book *Good to Great,* great companies build a consistent system with clear constraints to give their people freedom and responsibility within that framework. This encourages self-disciplined people who don't need to be managed as much. These companies focus more on managing systems, not people.

You want to build a high-performance growth mindset culture to sustain great results. Recent research shows that organisations with clearly engaged sales teams are 18% more effective than those with disengaged teams.[23]

We've covered off some critical areas to ensure you're retaining your top performers. Any one of these critical areas can trigger the loss of a quality professional, especially the loss of trust and respect. It can happen very fast.

CHAPTER 10

Training Your Hiring Managers

This is the best investment you can make for a new hiring manager, HR person or any manager who has influence with recruiting salespeople. Most of us have never received any formal training or guidance on how to attract, select and retain top talent. This chapter will walk you through our pathway to success. It's exciting.

We do a lot of work with our clients in this area. I always say that we can do as much or as little hiring training as you like because each company is different.

You can undertake the accredited STAR™ training course,[24] and we can consult with you on your search to attract top talent and/or provide you with support to select the best talent. We can do part of it up to the first interview stage, or we can do it all for you. If you have pressure on reducing costs and head count, we're here to help our clients in the best possible way.

The goal of the STAR™ training course is to hire salespeople that will be effective in selling your company's products and services. The STAR™ hiring system is easy to implement, saves time and is cost-effective.

There is a STAR™ training option available to suit different needs:

- **You recruit internally and you have a HR manager.** Potentially, they're busy. Juggling multiple tasks. Many clients we work with have multiple sites, and managers are also expected to recruit. And it's difficult to attract, find and select talent. STAR™ allows you to become certified, with access to all the processes, templates and the assessment tool to support your hiring process. You'll save time, money and utilise the system that has supported over 110,000 hires around the world.[25] It's the best investment you'll make to streamline you're hiring process and reduce hiring errors.

- **You don't have HR. You prefer to hire in-house and save money.** There is a fair chance that you're snowed under, juggling multiple balls, never been trained to recruit, and you've had a few false starts. This is a trap, I've been there.

Your company doesn't want to pay a recruiter, or potentially you don't have the capital to invest. Maybe you've had bad experiences in the past like me when I was a leader. Maybe you've already advertised and you haven't had great results.

You've either picked up the best of an average bunch or you're sitting on the fence, and your existing team is picking up some of the slack, but they're now getting stressed and you're struggling to keep them.

If this is the case, you can get STAR™ accreditation. We can support your hiring journey on a variety of budgets, it really depends on how much time you have, and budget.

Time is money, so we can provide automation, technology and tools to help you hire and attract better talent. It can be done over small, bite-sized sessions to work around your busy schedule and not dump more pressure onto you. It's a win-win. The long-term benefits will far outweigh the short-term challenges of allocating time for training. From our experience having completed this STAR™ training, it's an extremely valuable qualification to have on your resume for further career opportunities.

- **You have an external recruiter, but their past hires haven't been successful.**

  Maybe they're your preferred partner who has a long-term relationship with a company owner or leader, but it's not working anymore.

  Things have changed. But one thing hasn't—your need to get top-quality sales professionals on your team.

  Calls need to be made. Maybe you're on the hamster wheel where they've recruited somebody. They've failed. They've replaced that person, they've failed.

  It's left a bad taste in your mouth; let alone the money you've invested.

  Sometimes companies hang in there, irrespective of the quality they're getting because they feel like they need to get their money back. In the past, we've worked with clients to support their selection process with other recruiters. We will knock out more of their candidates but also save you valuable time avoiding interviewing ones that aren't a good fit and replacing ones that won't perform to your expectations. We can either assess individual candidates if you have a shortlist already, or, follow best practice and put them all through the sales DNA assessment. That is our recommendation.

This is where *Crystal Ball Recruiting* will help you. It will make you an expert in recruitment.

Recruitment is just part of what we do. We're also leaders in sales training, processes and technology implementation. We have a lot more buy-in with our clients. It's a long-term partnership for success.

Our process is unique. It's a combination of us personally hiring hundreds of salespeople for our clients, and STAR™ training has supported over 110,000 hires around the world. Over 30 years of hiring data is available at our fingertips.[26] It's powerful and it will change the way you recruit forever if you work with us.

We're always getting new technology and using better systems to create a more accurate hiring experience. If we can get your hiring to improve performance by 10 or 20%, then consider the impact on your bottom line. You won't need to fly blind or go on gut feel with your recruiting when you work with us because your team will be using a proven process that leads to success.

You will not only learn the 21 core competencies that drive measurable, scalable results, but you'll also gain access to all the templates and processes to guide your hiring managers. And if one of your managers leaves, their replacement can be trained to use the same systems and processes.

STAR™ Workshop

Learning objectives include:

- Understanding what makes hiring and managing salespeople fundamentally different.
- Using sales competency data to drive long-term performance improvement before you even hire someone.

You will be provided with:

- Access to predictive sales results to support your hiring decisions. This can identify gaps and development opportunities across your existing team.
- An easy-to-follow roadmap to support your recruitment.

The workshop is not a lecture, but more of a practical discussion.

Three Options to Utilise STAR™ Training to Suit Your Needs

1. A **one-day** virtual workshop.
2. **Five virtual 90-minute sessions** scheduled fortnightly on Wednesdays.
3. **8 virtual 60-minute sessions** scheduled each Wednesday.

Considering the cost of one bad hire, investing in STAR™ training will pay for itself.

If you would like team sessions, please confirm numbers and timelines to suit your business. It could be for a combination of hiring managers, sales managers, leaders and HR. We can customise a plan for your team.

Selected STAR™ Module Summaries

Here are examples of some modules you'll cover:

- **Module 1**
  The introduction to help you understand and optimise your recruitment process. We will look at the biggest challenges that you've faced when recruiting.

  We will look at your hiring readiness and ask questions to get a better understanding of where you're at now to encourage an open dialogue from the outset. There's no blaming and no excuses. We are just focused on trying to help fix problems and discussing your challenges. We explain how we use science and data to recruit.

- **Module 2**
  We go into detail about why your salespeople must be different and why your company has potentially struggled to hire top-quality salespeople.

Salespeople thrive under pressure, unlike most roles, so success does depend on handling competition, timing, and overcoming resistance. Research shows that your top 16% of salespeople potentially drive 80% of your business.[27]

We will look at why your past hires have failed, discuss traits of your A-players, and the potential flaws and cost of recruitment issues.

- **Module 3**
  The job description. Remember the stat from Chapter 8 that 70% of new hires say that their job was misrepresented to them?[28]

  The Society of Human Resource Management estimates that over 50% of new hires leave within the first six months because of inaccurate job descriptions. They recommend updating job descriptions at least twice per year.[29]

  Our goal for job descriptions is to focus on leading KPI outcomes, not just tasks.

  We will review and compare sample job description templates and align this with your performance expectations.

  A hiring manager must own the job description, but cross-department input is vital. An inaccurate job description leads to misaligned expectations.

- **Module 4**
  We will investigate why top talent seeks top-rated workplaces. Research shows that over 80% of candidates research a company's reputation before deciding whether to apply.[30]

  We will look at best practices for your business to maximise its strengths. We will also help you to develop authentic messaging to align with what current top performers want to experience in a new job.

- **Module 5**
  Writing your job ad. Our goal is to help you write a job ad that attracts top sales performers. Your ad should inspire them to apply.

  We want quality over quantity. We focus on candidate needs and headlines that grab top performer's attention like an impacting movie or email title.

  You will be provided with templates to craft compelling job ads. We will get feedback and compare your draft ads to competitors to make sure you stand out in your environment.

- **Module 6**
  Sourcing is the process of attracting and generating candidates. It's critical to target passive top performers when talent is scarce. We can help you

utilise our AI sales talent identification tools and network to source and attract more talent, not order-takers.

The assessment tool will accurately predict top performers very early and will reduce bias in hiring.

Other Selected STAR™ Module Topics

They include:

- A structured phone screen and scorecard to ensure consistency and efficiency.
- How to conduct structured interviews, including templates, processes and systems to help you.
- Best-practice reference checking.
- 30/60/90-day onboarding with success plans.
- How to effectively interpret our sales candidate assessments.
- Sales manager recruitment.

If you've enjoyed my first book, then buy a copy for your HR manager, your sales manager or any other hiring managers who could benefit from STAR™ training. It will make you a lot of money. It's a practical tool for all current and new managers. They all need it in their toolbox. I wish I'd had this opportunity many years ago as a hiring manager.

Finally, please jump onto Google, Amazon or any other leading platform and leave us a book review. We love feedback.

Afterword

When I began writing *Crystal Ball Recruiting*, I didn't set out to write just another book about hiring salespeople. I wanted to challenge the status quo—to help leaders stop guessing and start recruiting with clarity, confidence and purpose.

Now that the book is complete, I'm struck by how many stories, strategies and lessons came together to form something bigger than I imagined. This isn't just a guide—it's a movement for recruitment, stronger teams and measurable ROI.

Throughout this journey, I've heard from leaders who've shifted their hiring mindset, HR managers who've redefined their criteria, and sales professionals who've found roles that truly fit. That's the impact I hoped for, and it's only the beginning.

If this book has helped you rethink how you hire, evaluate or lead your sales team, then I invite you to stay connected:

- Access additional resources via https://jasonhowes.com.au/book/downloads.
- Subscribe to the *Sales Trajectory* podcast.
- Connect on LinkedIn or Instagram.
- Leave a quick review on Amazon, Google or our website.
- Know someone who'd benefit? Share the book—it might be the game-changer they need.

Thank you for reading and being part of this journey.

Speaker Bio

Jason Howes isn't just a speaker—he's in the trenches every day actively hunting for new business and leading from the front. He knows the pressure, the pace and the persistence it takes to succeed in sales and recruitment because he lives it.

As Managing Director of Arrow Executive Sales, Jason brings over 35 years of hands-on experience in new business development, sales leadership and recruitment. He's the author *of Crystal Ball Recruitment* and host of the *Sales Trajectory* podcast, where he explores how top sales performers are built—not born.

Jason is a lifelong student of the game, constantly refining his craft and sharing that journey with sales leaders and professionals. His sessions are outcome-driven, packed with real-world insights, and designed to deliver maximum value to every audience.

With a speaking style that blends strategy, storytelling and humour, Jason makes complex ideas feel practical and inspiring. If you're looking for a high-impact speaker or facilitator for your next sales conference, then book Jason Howes. He'll equip your team with the tools to be stronger leaders and to grow faster. His dedication to sales excellence always delivers a return on investment.

Offers

THE VAULT – offer 1

Unlock the knowledge that powers top sales teams.

What's Inside

- Exclusive access to our blogs, published articles, and white papers
- On-demand webinar recordings featuring top sales insights
- Private access to additional sales leadership recordings
- Monthly newsletter with innovative strategies, tools, and stories from the field

Why It Matters

Whether you are a sales leader, recruiter, or business owner, The Vault gives you the edge to:

- Stay ahead of industry trends
- Learn from real-world recruiting wins and mistakes
- Build trust and authority in your hiring decisions

Access The Vault Now

THE VAULT Unlock the knowledge
that powers top sales teams

www.jasonhowes.com.au/books/downloads

Unlock the Secrets of Top Sales Teams

PERFORMANCE PULSE – offer 2

Check in. Diagnose. Decide.

Gain instant clarity with the Sales DNA assessment. Whether you're hiring, evaluating a team member, or planning performance improvements, Performance Pulse delivers fast, science-backed insights to guide your decisions. Results available within 24 hours, with 95% accurate insights.

Your Sales Team's Health Check – Today and Tomorrow.

Use Cases for Leaders:

- Quickly assess shortlisted candidates you're unsure about.
- Diagnose performance issues in current team members.

- Use data-driven insights to guide coaching and development.
- Make confident hiring and promotion decisions.

www.jasonhowes.com.au/books/downloads

Mention Crystal Ball Recruiting, leave us a Google Review to qualify for 15% off your first transaction.

STAR™ RECRUITMENT SYSTEM– offer 3

Train your team to hire like experts.

Learn the **STAR™** system, bring recruitment back in-house, and build a repeatable process to attract and hire top-tier sales professionals. Save up to 50% if you're using an external recruiter.

You'll get all the systems, templates and ensure your team saves time and money to interview the best fit for your role criteria without bias getting in the way.

Whether you are a leader or hiring manager, **STAR™** will:

- Navigate the full **STAR™** methodology step by step
- Ensure only recommended candidates proceed to interviewing stage
- Remove inconsistency in your hiring decisions

STAR™ virtual options:

- A one-day workshop
- 5 x 90 min sessions
- 8 x 60 min sessions

CTA: Book Your workshop in now

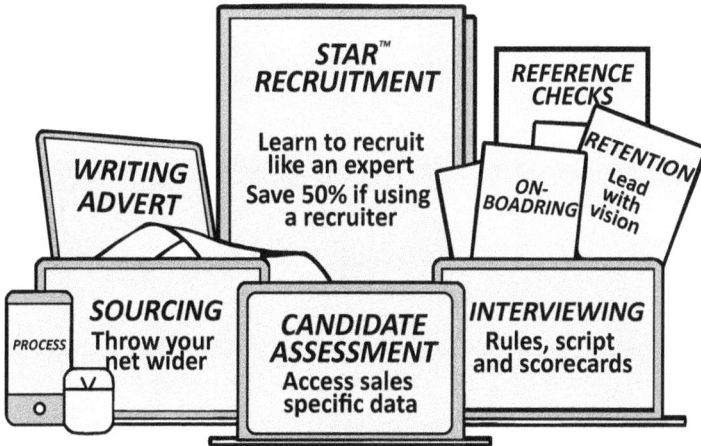

www.jasonhowes.com.au/books/downloads

Endnotes

1   https://blog.hubspot.com/sales/how-to-manage-a-high-performing-sales-team

2   https://medium.com/geekculture/50-of-all-sales-hires-fail-why-62f130cc6b6a

3   https://www.inc.com/tim-askew/why-sales-hires-fail-75-of-the-time-within-the-first-year.html

4   https://www.objectivemanagement.com/

5   Ibid.

6   Ibid.

7   https://www.quotapath.com/blog/compensation-planning-feedback/

8   https://professionalprograms.mit.edu/blog/design/why-95-of-new-products-miss-the-mark-and-how-yours-can-avoid-the-same-fate/

9   https://www.salesforce.com/au/blog/15-sales-statistics/

10 https://www.objectivemanagement.com/

11 https://talent.seek.com.au/hiring-advice/article/why-you-should-be-keeping-a-close-eye-on-your-job-ad

12 https://www.forbes.com/sites/heidilynnekurter/2019/10/29/yale-exposes-new-bias-that-judges-interviewees-within-first-few-seconds-of-interview/

13 https://www.objectivemanagement.com/

14 Ibid.

15   Ibid.

16   https://www.forbes.com/councils/forbestechcouncil/
      2022/07/20/why-poor-onboarding-and-training-is-causing-
      sales-reps-to-leave-their-jobs/

17   https://www.forbes.com/sites/bryanrobinson/2024/06/20/
      study-reveals-why-70-of-hiring-managers-lie-to-job-
      candidates-in-2024/

18   https://www.ahri.com.au/resources-2/hr-research/the-
      state-of-wellbeing-in-australian-workplaces-2019-2022

19   https://www.forbes.com/sites/randyillig/2024/08/29/10-
      tips-to-onboard-new-sales-hires-effectively/

20   https://www.objectivemanagement.com/

21   https://blog.orbispay.me/82-of-managers-arent-the-right-fit/

22   https://www.gallup.com/workplace/236579/one-people-
      possess-talent-manage.aspx

23   https://www.gallup.com/workplace/285674/improve-
      employee-engagement-workplace.aspx

24   https://www.objectivemanagement.com/

25   Ibid.

26   Ibid.

27   Ibid.

28   https://www.forbes.com/sites/bryanrobinson/2024/06/20/
      study-reveals-why-70-of-hiring-managers-lie-to-job-
      candidates-in-2024/

29   https://www.shrm.org/topics-tools/news/talent-acquisition/
      new-hires-skip-role-doesnt-meet-expectations

30   https://www.glassdoor.com/blog/most-important-employer-
      branding-statistics/

*This research has been provided by Objective Management Group and is
shared with permission. www.objectivemanagement.com*

Notes

CRYSTAL BALL RECRUITING

_____

_____

_____

_____

_____

_____

_____

_____

_____

_____

_____

_____

_____

_____

NOTES

NOTES

CRYSTAL BALL RECRUITING

NOTES